To : A

MW00677396

ALEXANDER
— THE —
COPPERSMITH

10/3 /2016

Kris A. Nordbender

Philippians 1: 6

ALEXANDER
THE
COPPERSMITH

KRIS A. NORDLANDER

TATE PUBLISHING
AND **ENTERPRISES**, LLC

Published by Tate Publishing & Enterprises, LLC
127 E. Trade Center Terrace | Mustang, Oklahoma 73064 USA
1.888.361.9473 | www.tatepublishing.com

Tate Publishing is committed to excellence in the publishing industry. The company reflects the philosophy established by the founders, based on Psalm 68:11,
"The Lord gave the word and great was the company of those who published it."

Book design copyright © 2016 by Tate Publishing, LLC. All rights reserved.
Cover design by Joshua Rafols
Interior design by Shieldon Alcasid

Published in the United States of America

ISBN: 978-1-68319-307-4
1. Religion / Christian Ministry / Missions
2. Religion / Christian Ministry / Evangelism
16.08.25

DEDICATION TO
THESE HOLY SCRIPTURES

Alexander the coppersmith did me much harm; the Lord will repay him according to his deeds. (2 Timothy 4:14)

Be on guard against him yourself, for he vigorously opposed our teaching. (2 Timothy 4:15)

For Demas having loved this present world has deserted me. (2 Timothy 4:10)

You are aware of the fact that all who are in Asia turned away from me, among whom are Phygelus and Hermogenes. (2 Timothy 1:15)

Therefore, do not be ashamed of the testimony of our Lord, or of me his prisoner; but join with me in suffering according to the power of God. (2 Timothy 1:8)

Requite them according to their work and according to the evil of their practices; Requite them according to the deeds of their hands; Repay them their recompense. (Psalm 28:4)

Let this be the reward of my accusers from the Lord, and those who speak evil against my soul. (Psalm 109:20)

The Lord says to my Lord: Sit at my right hand Until I make Your enemies a footstool for Your feet. (Psalm 110:1)

But even if we, or an angel of heaven, should preach to you a gospel contrary to what we have preached to you, he is to be accursed. (Galatians 1:8)

Whenever you stand praying, forgive, if you have anything against anyone, so that your Father who is in heaven will also forgive your transgressions. (Mark 11:25)

Acknowledgments

To THE GLORY of God the Father, Jesus Christ, His work on the cross, the power of His resurrection, His work in the world, and the work of the Holy Spirit.

To my beloved wife, who faithfully withstood persecution, along with my small children, who knew nothing about the battle.

To the true church of Jesus Christ, which lives and follows the only true Christ Jesus.

To the ministers, missionaries, and workers who have been persecuted and accused falsely in modern-day times.

For God's glory and the upholding of scriptural evangelism and truth in a day where society is looking for cultural salvation and believers are afraid to share their faith.

For Christians who are tired of self-help and sincerely desire the fullness of God in these times.

For this reason it says, "Awake, sleeper, and arise from the dead, and Christ will shine on you."

—Ephesians 5:14

ABOUT THE AUTHOR

ALEXANDER THE COPPERSMITH combines stories of real activities on the home field and foreign mission field in a third-world country. After being converted and transformed by Jesus Christ in the early 1980s, Kris started a lifelong journey of pursuing God or, rather, God pursuing him.

God moved him in the direction of frontline evangelism among Moslems. Through the process of events, personal crisis, and the teaching of godly men, Kris learned truths about false religion, demonic activities, and how to present the gospel to people ensnared in hard-line Islam.

Kris has been in fourteen different countries around the world. At the time of writing this book, he was sharing the gospel of Jesus Christ in Chad, Democratic Republic of Congo, and Mexico, where the need is great for evangelical churches and trained believers and the laborers are few.

Kris was born and raised in Colorado. He holds a BA in pastoral studies from Colorado Christian University and an MA in ministry from Luther Rice Seminary. He has been a missionary since 1991, along with Nancy, his wife. Kris speaks three languages other than English. Kris and his wife, Nancy, have five adopted children. They also have a ministry to orphans and teenagers as the Lord has brought children into their lives over the years. Praise God and give Him glory!

Kris and his family continue to pray that many people will come to know Jesus Christ as their Savior, Lord, and Life until the rapture. Pray with them:

> I keep asking that the God of our Lord Jesus Christ, the glorious Father, may give you the Spirit of wisdom and revelation, so that you may know him better. I pray also that the eyes of your heart may be enlightened in order that you may know the hope to which he has called you, the riches of the glorious inheritance in the saints, and his incomparably great power for us who believe. That power is like the working of his mighty strength. (Ephesians 1:17–19)

CONTENTS

PREFACE

TIME IS IRRELEVANT when it comes to living and working in God's power. Only God's timing is relevant. The church spends most of its time on worldly methods or the newest fad. Modern-day Christian enterprise in the United States, for the most part, has ended up as was foretold by Frances Schaeffer in his book section titled "When the Church Becomes Like the World." The missionary enterprise has followed the counsel of modern-day methods. Seminary degrees, although important, cannot replace a man or woman "sold out" to Jesus Christ. The enterprise has trusted in false gods like psychology, entertainment, cultural training, and financial extravagance to make its practice known at the expense of fasting, prayer, and the study of the holy scriptures. Dr. John F. MacArthur calls it pragmatism. Jesus Christ said, "The flesh profits little, it is the Spirit who gives life" (John 6:63).

God's way is still better. John the Baptist understood victory and prepared the way for God's Son. It is the person surrendered to God who is rewarded in this life with quality and the life in paradise to come. The quality of one

Christian surrendered outweighs any material or financial benefit of this present world. It is when Jesus Christ is not only preached as Savior and Lord but as the very sustenance of life, "reigning in life" (Romans 5:17). Faithful and true missionary enterprise is accomplished through God's mighty power.

Persecution does exist for faithful brethren who are sold out to the evangelistic message of Jesus Christ. In this book, a real-life account brings truth, meaning, and story to the reader. It is true. The names have been changed to protect both those trapped and ensnared in evil and those who have trusted Christ Jesus for eternal salvation. After all, they both shall be brought to justice on that day, "for each one of us will give an account of himself to God" (Romans 14:12). The church needs to preserve the truth of Scripture in these last days before the rapture and tribulation.

1

NEW LIFE

IT WAS IN the late 1970s that I began to reflect about my life. Oh yes, I had a best friend who drowned in the eighth grade. I kept awake all night for about a week and had to climb into my parents' bed. The trouble was that he perished because he could not swim. The water in Colorado was so cold that year in the spring; and there I was, night after night, in horror, thinking I could save him because I was on the swim team. Swimming was no problem for me, and Steve jumped off the wood raft on a windswept lake, fearing he would perish. During those long nights, I had a hard time sleeping because of his death. I even told my parents that he came and talked with me while I was sitting on a lawn chair in the front yard. Now I know this was a demonic spirit who reflected him and deceived me.

My grandmother on my mother's side died. My parents and relatives on my mother's side went to the funeral together. There was a good gospel message presented, but to my knowledge at the time, there were no brethren there. I was really upset at a young age of seventeen, obviously because I had no hope. It became known later for me that death, although real, escapes the conscience and is avoided. Some reflection was done for a month or so about where I would spend eternity. When I grew up, the Bible had little importance. The teaching of a personal relationship with Jesus Christ was not practiced.

I had been to church camp and heard the gospel message when I was about ten years old. I even made an intellectual profession of faith, which didn't change me. There wasn't any follow-up that may or may not have made any difference in protecting me from the foolishness to come. I was a fool. I knew some real Christians next door, the Smiths, older people whom my parents misunderstood, who gave me my first Bible. I kept it fresh and new, hidden in a box of keepsakes until I was born again some ten years later. It was worth the wait, but not worth the battle to finally open it and read it. The Smiths did their best to inform me of the truth, but my eyes were blinded and deceived even more because of witchcraft at a "Halloween" event at a liberal church when I was around ten. She brought me in, this witch, to do a fingernail work. The drape-enclosed room had lit candles. It was dark, and the woman said some things to me that I didn't understand. I knew later what curses were because I was given the ability to understand the truth.

Sure, I was a good kid until my senior year in high school. I played sports and all those activities, but I was rejected by the baseball coach. Coaches always have their pets, and Dave Goodwin was our coach's pet. Our pitchers were wild, and as I caught their fastballs in the dirt, it was very difficult to be perfect. One time, a pitcher threw about fifteen consecutive dirt-ball pitches. I missed two of them, and the coach took me out of the game, and of course, he put in Dave. Guess what? Dave missed more wild pitches as a catcher, and the opposite team scored big time. The coach looked really embarrassed that his pet had failed. He put me back in the game reluctantly but desperately.

The score was held to only Dave's passed balls. Something changed about my attitude because of many rejections. Although I was a sinner by nature and choice, I hurt immensely on the inside. Christianity was available, but the only real Christian I knew who lived the life or, rather, let Christ live through him was my grandfather. I wrestled with being accepted all my life. Moreover, since I was not accepted by any level of society, I quietly hurt inside from deep rejection growing up. The rejections were many, which I will not explain now, but I would later be delivered from them by the power of the Holy Spirit. The Bible is true when it says, "And do not be conformed to this world, but be *transformed by the renewing of your mind*, so that you may prove what the will of God is, that which is good acceptable and perfect" (Romans 12:2).

In college, I tried marijuana and turned professional alcohol guzzler during parties. Alcohol would be the setback of my life previous to my new life in Christ Jesus. Alcohol and drugs only soothe hurt feelings and block reality from a convicted conscience that God is real and that there is a need for a relationship with him that is holy. At the time, I thought I was having fun because certain sins always do that. Flag football, skiing, friends, and partying were my life during that time. After all the fun, I know I am blessed to be here. Studying was something I did because I paid for it as my parents were not able to help much. And when I flunked my first college biology test, it really scared me. Many efforts were made to improve, but the tests were hard, and once again, failure stood knocking at my door. At night and on weekends, it was the accepted thing for everyone to "get fried" during the late sixties and early seventies.

My friends were there, and we found pleasure in just being students with an agenda to party. Nothing—study, work, or play—had a final goal except to escape reality. Rock and roll was the music of the day. Van Halen, Uriah Heep, Pink Floyd, Jethro Tull, and many others captivated my heart and mind further into darkness. At school, there were a few who proclaimed they were Christians, but I was never witnessed to by any of them. I can only credit God sending His angels on my behalf because He was knocking at the door of my heart. My friends rejected me later on.

My relatives never confronted me on my problems much, but would I have changed had they done so? We don't know. It would be years before I even knew the word *sovereignty* and understood it. Some said they were Christians, but they watched television shows and laughed just as heartily as I did at the off-color jokes. I had to leave my party friends at college because I knew it just was not working out. Nevertheless, I continued this way of life off and on for about ten years, wondering about deliverance. I always wanted to quit the party scene, but I was in bondage to sin and death.

Since I was a phony, I saw most Christians as phonies too. Later, I really wanted help because I was tired of my actions and the way life was going. I got scared of dying and what the outcome would be. Where would I be?

Going about my business and working hard physically were things I felt I could accomplish. I dreamed of being very successful in the business world. I could remodel, weld, do plumbing—my earthly father had been an electrician. All these natural skills and talents would be used when God called on me to use them. They would all be needed in the future because I was going to Africa, learn several languages, and be on frontline evangelism. Are you kidding me?

Review: True Salvation

1. The results of true salvation are a changed life and a new direction (repentance) and assurance of eternal life (John 3:3, John 14:6, 1 John 5:10–13).

2. Assurance of salvation is based on the trustworthiness of God and His Word, the confirmation of the Holy Spirit, and a changed life (2 Timothy 3:16, Romans 8:16, Romans 6:22).

3. When someone becomes a believer, their relationship to old friends may change (2 Timothy 2:19).

4. Family members will either like your new life or may think you are a religious radical (Job 2:9–13).

2

Bringing in the Blind

My grandmother became blind at the end of her life. A diabetic coma added to her illness of diabetes. In the early 1980s, I knew I had enough of a turmoil in life. Although I didn't know it, I was blind spiritually. God began to reveal Himself to me through loving people. I always remembered my grandfather on my dad's side, who—although he was not a preacher—lived holy. Never did I want to offend him in any way. During a hospital stay, I was attended to by an aide who did not share Christ verbally, but I sensed the same thing in her as I did with my grandfather. It was Christ living through her life (Galatians 2:20).

I came home from a hard day's physical work to relax and watch television. During those times before salvation, I spent many afternoons watching David Carradine on *Kung Fu*. *Kung Fu* was intriguing to me at the time when I was searching for answers in my disappointing life. The source of the program *Kung Fu* was found in Taoism (Quan Zhen Religion), "a principal philosophy and system of religion of China based on the teachings of Lao-tzu in the sixth century B.C."[1] Countless times, I would turn on the television and watch *The Big Valley*, a Western. I can recall during one of the shows the verse "Do not urge me to leave you or turn back from following you; for where you go, I will go, and where you lodge, I will lodge. Your people shall be my people, and your God, my God" (Ruth 1:16). It was as if a powerful voice was speaking to me, reminding me of the days long past when I had some influence from the Word of God.

Because of these incidences, I was drawn to spiritual counseling through a person who worked for Campus Crusade for Christ. Joel led me to an older pastor who shared with me how to be set free from the power of sin's domination. The pastor-counselor laid hands on me and prayed that I would be healed from the top of my head to the bottom of my feet. I came across that first Bible the Smiths had given me years earlier. I began reading in 1 Corinthians chapter 6:9–11. It says,

> Or do you not know that the unrighteous will not inherit the kingdom of God? Do not be deceived; neither fornicators, nor idolaters, nor adulterers, nor effeminate, nor homosexuals, nor thieves, nor the covetous, nor drunkards, nor revilers, nor swindlers,

> will inherit the kingdom of God. Such were some of
> you; but you were washed, but you were sanctified,
> but you were justified in the name of the Lord Jesus
> Christ and in the Spirit of our God.

The Holy Spirit was convincing me of my hopeless and loss state. After that, God saved me in my car. Not only did my physical organs need to be healed but also my soul. The word *salvation* means "to heal" and, in like manner, "to mend." Repentance and belief in the Lord Jesus Christ had taken place in my life (Romans 10:9–10). For the next few months, I would ask myself, What is this? I'm different now. I see things from a new perspective—God's perspective.

Little did I know how difficult things would become because of God's saving power. My father rejected me immediately upon becoming a Christian. He was like all the other professing Christians I met who said, "I did that a long time ago" when speaking of believing in Christ. What my dad meant by his statement was that he hoped he would go to heaven, but his life was not changed. He was so upset by my testimony, and he said I was crazy. In fact, I was so different that it was hard for people to believe that I was really myself.

Other distant family members accepted the fact that I was different. George believed I needed a change, but he still went about his alcohol and drug habits as usual. I shared the faith in Jesus Christ with him. I believe it scared him so much, the change that God had made in me, that he became bewildered. To this day, I believe his life is a mess. I told most of my college friends the good news about what Christ had done for me and accepted the fact that God had changed me, but they were not ready for God to change them. One friend told me, "At least you're not telling people they are going to hell."

There is one truth my pastoral counselor insisted on me understanding. He insisted that I give my whole life to God in Christ Jesus. Romans 12:1–2 says,

> Therefore I urge you by the mercies of God, to present your bodies a living and holy sacrifice, acceptable to God, which is your spiritual service of worship. And do not be conformed to this world, but be transformed by the renewing of your mind, that you may prove what the will of God is, that which is good and acceptable and perfect.

At the time, I didn't experience or understand all the ramifications of this verse. I knew that it would require giving up control of my 1950 Studebaker, which I loved. I didn't know that God would change my whole life's direction and vocation.

God brought me out of darkness and into His light. After I believed in the Lord Jesus, God took me through a downer. I lost control of everything and everybody. Charles Solomon, in his book *The Ins and Outs of Rejection*, best puts it this way,

> If a person at this point of complete surrender is all
> the way to the end of himself and the Holy Spirit
> reveals to him the corruptness of self or the flesh,
> he is ready to claim by faith his identification with
> Christ. He has been fighting it all the way and he
> finally lets go in complete surrender and God meets
> him and revolutionizes his life. God accepts the
> surrender, reveals the indwelling Christ, and the
> person is set free. When a person is at the bottom
> he can't go any lower and God reaches him there.[2]

God stripped everything away from me that I had always
trusted in, including myself. In the inside of my life were
insecurities, anxieties, and inadequacies. When God broke me,
He set me free for the very first time from a reliance on all these
negative strongholds. I began to experience deep peace even
when all things were going wrong. I lost my house and barely
hung on to my business. I had to move into an apartment. I
started reading the Scriptures and praying for long hours. For
two years, I turned off the television and spent time with God.
I was single at the time having no other responsibilities. It was
the power of the Holy Spirit working in me.

Through the scriptures, there was a realization that my
whole life before accepting Jesus Christ was a waste of
time. I rarely read the newspaper. I really did not care about
anything. I just worked my way through life, hoping that
it would turn out all right before I met the Savior of the
world. Now I was set free.

Review: Salvation, Identification, and Total Commitment

1. True salvation is a result of the power of God transforming one's spirit into a God-filled spirit (John 3:3, 1 Corinthians 12:13, 2 Corinthians 5:17, Acts1:8, Ezekiel 11:19).

2. Flesh or sin singular is the carnal nature of man that controls the nonbeliever and is a force or power that the Christian is warring against through the power of the Holy Spirit. Even though a Christian dies to the power of sin, sin does not die (Romans 6:1–23). All Christians have victory in Christ, but that victory needs to be understood and appropriated through the power of the Holy Spirit daily (Ephesians 2:6, Galatians 5:15–26).

3. Identification is a true understanding of one's eternal position in Christ Jesus, both intellectual and experimental. Understanding cocrucifixion, coburial, and coresurrection, and the cross as an instrument of death are crucial to being delivered from the power of sin (Luke 9:23–25, Romans 6:6, Galatians 2:20).

4. Dying to self is an initial "deathblow," with a continuous effect of dying daily (Luke 9:23).

5. A prayer of total commitment allows God the right to begin a powerful and wonderful work in a Christian's life, resulting in brokenness and transformation (Romans 12:1–2).

6. The result of brokenness and suffering is a godly faith and witness, the filling of the Holy Spirit (Acts 1:8).

3

MISSIONARY EXAMPLES

GOD HAS AN exact timing when His work is to be accomplished. His perfect will is not completed as it would have been before the fall of man in the garden. However, when salvation comes to the believer and he or she surrenders to God without reservation, His good and perfect will can be accomplished (Romans 12:1–3). God has a timetable as it pertains to foreseeable events that will take place. He has a plan in mind. His plan is for your salvation if you believe and the salvation of every people group, tongue, tribe, and nation as they believe. His word is true as He gave Abraham the promise in Genesis 12:3: "And in you all the families of the earth shall be blessed."

As I was studying the scriptures, the Holy Spirit brought to my attention Acts 9:15–16. It says,

> But the Lord said to him, "Go, for he is a chosen instrument of mine, to bear My name before the Gentiles and kings and the sons of Israel; for I will show him how much he will suffer for My name's sake."

I believe that this was for the apostle Paul. However, the Holy Spirit started convincing me that in some way, fashion, or form, I would be sharing the gospel in some large scale. The part of the verse I did not like reading was the "how much he will suffer for My name's sake." The odds of this happening were very slim. Although I finished high school and went to college for two years, I had no motivation to study anything. How would a simple, ordinary person like me be ready for such a large challenge?

Have you read the famous missionary biographies of old Christianity? I started reading them. The first book that got my attention was *Hudson Taylor's Spiritual Secret*. The story goes into great detail how Hudson Taylor as a missionary worked in foreign lands in his own strength until God revealed to him that it was to be Christ living through his life (Galatians 2:20). As I read that book, the Holy Spirit again made me wrestle with a personal call to begin sharing the gospel of Jesus Christ.

Nevertheless, how could a person so low in academic performance and new to the church actually be called? My contact with born-again Christians had been minimal.

As I started to attend church and hear the preaching and teaching of Dr. Joe, I was still being convicted to become a missionary. In addition, I do not forget all those times I turned on the radio when Dr. John MacArthur was preaching great truths that pertained to God's call and suffering. Those were the days before the technical world developed.

If you are called to preach the gospel, it only corresponds that you must pray. I heard of the books *Praying Hyde Intercessor* by Reese Howell and *Prayer Life* by Andrew Murray and then read them. After reading the books, I realized that my prayer life was not anything close to the kind of shape it needed to be, whether as a Christian missionary or not. The most convincing statement of these books was, "Prayerlessness is sin." Therefore, I made it a point to start my day early and pray for all those in my life who needed God. My focus is and was always on what God would do through prayer.

Finally, God used a book on my life about C. T. Studd. It was there that I read about Africa from a Christian perspective. It was C. T. Studd's testimony that convinced me to surrender the life of the world that I was accustomed to in exchange for the life of a third-world missionary. After all, what would my relatives think? Would everyone think I was so different to go to Africa and maybe even die? I could only conclude as Hudson Taylor did, "I've already died."

> Knowing this that our old self was crucified with him, that our body of sin might be done away with, that we should no longer be slaves to sin. (Romans 6:6)

> I have been crucified with Christ; and it is no longer I who live, but Christ lives in me; and the life which I now live in the flesh I live by faith in the Son of God, who loved me, and delivered Himself up for me. (Galatians 2:20)

This meant that I could not live for selfish ambition. This meant that my call was real. It was not because I grew up in a Christian home. This meant that I could not rely on all the Christian clichés and beliefs of self-preservation. It meant that I was called by the true and living God of the universe. How humbling would that be? Besides, who would believe this call? I did not know anyone. I was not well recognized in the church. In fact, I did not yet have a Bible and seminary education. Who would believe me? The answer is God.

Because of this, one day I made an appointment with my pastor Dr. JJ. My question was this, "How do you know you are called to the gospel ministry?" His response was, "Through the Word of God." He also gave me some recommendations on what Christian schooling I needed and all these important decisions. But how could I pass Bible college? Since I dropped out of college years earlier, I never read anything, including the newspaper. Was this possible? Most likely not!

Then I read a book by George Mueller. George Mueller operated an orphanage and did God's work by the power of prayer, glorifying God. I recall a story how his orphanage children needed food. In answer to prayer, sacks of potatoes were brought to his door. Someone had heard of this need indirectly and brought the potatoes. Again, his secret to success in life and ministry was prayer to God's glory.

I attended a Christian seminar where all kinds of ministries were presented in open forum. Each group had a table of important information about their ministries. The day I attended, there was a mission work that presented Guatemala. I phoned the leader of the group and asked if I could participate in a two-week mission. For about a month, I had not received a response from him. Each day, I would pray about that trip. Finally, I took my first short-term mission trip to Guatemala. It was a new experience for me to make a trip to a foreign land. God continued working with me about my call to third-world missions.

After I returned to the United States, I wrestled with the choice of learning French or Spanish. Eventually I would learn both languages as God arranged the travel plans of my life. I also wrestled with going to a Spanish-speaking country or Africa. God led me to Africa.

It was during this time that I made a commitment to go to Africa as a faith missionary. Because of C. T. Studd's book and Acts 9:15–16, I knew I was called to Africa. If God was going to send me there, then He alone would have to provide the church, the people, and money to go there by faith. I really did not even know where in Africa I would be heading. At this time in my life, I did not know one personal living example of a real missionary. It was only when I started praying that God began to reveal His perfect will. Little did I know that, later in life, I would be going to the Democratic Republic of the Congo, where C. T. Studd began his missionary work, and I would be preaching the gospel to those in Sanda.

Later on, I would hear the testimony of Jim Elliot through his wife, Elisabeth Elliot, and be confronted with the possibility of persecution. Jim Elliot had been martyred at the hands of the Auca Indian tribe in Ecuador, South America.

By the way, prayer is work. Some say the average ordained minister in the Unites States spends four minutes a day in prayer. If God's work is to be done, let it be bathed in prayer.

Review: Missionary Examples

1. God calls His people to salvation and service (Ephesians 2:1–10).

2. When Christians are sensitive to the leading of the Holy Spirit, He guides when and where a Christian is to work and serve (Romans 8:14, John 10:3).

3. God calls the church to go into all the world and make disciples. He also calls individuals to use their spiritual gifts to accomplish world evangelism. (Matthew 28:19–20, 1 Corinthians 12:4).

4. It is evident by the testimonies of many missionaries—the Greek word *apostolos* means "sent ones"—that God is active in preparing men and woman to service all over the world.

5. A God-called apostle is one who spends his life preaching the gospel in places where there is yet to be a witness and in difficult areas of the world. This is a spiritual gift now called missionary by the modern church. Going on a mission trip does not make one an apostle or a missionary in this sense. It is a separate calling and gifting by God given to start work where no one else dares to go.

4

THE FINGER OF GOD

TRUSTING IN THE Almighty One, who inhabits eternity, is a process. Most people depend on their education to get a position or to move ahead in the world. It was hard to imagine that God could use me to cast out demons. Remember, I was a new Christian, only having been in a relationship with Him about four years. I had read the Bible thoroughly for that same amount of time. I took Bible correspondence courses. I decided to go to Bible college but had not yet finished that degree.

A young woman in our church seemed to be struggling. She had been involved in the occult and a sinful lifestyle. God used another woman, a man of God, and me in her life. God had raised up this man of God to do work in counseling and to teach spiritual warfare. This man of God had also done work in exorcisms.

Through meeting at a church ministry, this young woman became more vocal in her distaste for my being there. It was not really her but the demons speaking against Christ in me. I spent about a month in prayer for her along with my regular prayer routine. Through a period of about two weeks, she came to the other woman for help. I called the man of God on spiritual warfare, and we made an appointment to meet together in the apartment I was renting.

The woman and I went to the young woman's house before our appointment. We sat down to lead her to Christ. As she trusted Christ as her Savior and Lord, I commanded unknown spirits to leave her alone in the name of Jesus Christ. As I prayed, her cat screamed with rage, clawing down the screen door on the outside porch. I had never seen anything so wild in my life. It must have been the cat being on the receiving end of demons that were intending to hide from Jesus Christ. Either that or Christ sent them into that cat.

Days later, we began the counseling sessions to cast away the evil spirits that were present in the young woman. All of a sudden, she got up and went into the bedroom for no apparent reason. I became alarmed because in the closet was a loaded .38 snub-nosed special Smith and Wesson. I had thoughts that she would be coming out with that loaded gun and kill all three of us. After about three separate four-hour sessions, the demons came out of her. We had fasted, prayed, and read scriptures concerning the fate of these demons. Finally the demons were all cast out with the finger of God and in the name of Jesus Christ and by Jesus Christ. "But if I cast out demons with the finger of God, then the Kingdom of God has come upon you" (Luke 11:20).

We asked the woman not to report this to the elders of the church where we were attending. She did so anyway. We really do not know the outcome of her testimony to them. The pastor grew up on a mission field as a missionary kid, so it did not surprise him in the least.

After that meeting, the young woman had counseling sessions with the man of God. It was there at the church ministry that I started a relationship with my wife-to-be. We had the most important thing in common—the Lord Jesus Christ as the central focus and master of our lives. Months following, we were married. Both of us believed God had called us to be foreign missionaries. God invested in our training so that we could face the difficult challenges of living in a third-world country and to face the spiritual warfare in dealing with Islam.

Our favorite missionary story was none other than that about Jim Elliot. Elisabeth Elliot wrote a book about the true missionary experience of martyrdom in the hands of the Auca Indians. Jim Elliot and four others were martyred at the hands of the Auca Indian tribe in Ecuador. Their names are Pete Fleming, Nate Saint, Ed McCully, and Roger Youderian. It was because of the book *Shadow of the Almighty: The Life and Testament of Jim Elliot* by Elisabeth Elliot that my wife and I are missionaries to this day.

At our wedding, we used a quote by Jim Elliot as he prepared to go to the foreign mission field. This quote is one that we still think about often as we ponder how God used it so that we could bring the gospel to North African Moslems. Many, for the first time, heard the gospel there because of Jim's testimony, Elisabeth's book, and our willingness to go. We had no idea that we too would be persecuted and still live through it.

> Lord, make my way prosperous, not that I achieve high station, but that my life would exhibit the value of knowing God.[3]

Review: The Finger of God

1. Demonic possession is still real, and miracles have not gone away as many say (Mark 5:1–20).

2. Exorcism is done by those gifted by the Holy Spirit (1 Corinthians 12:10) and by the power of the Holy Spirit in the name of Jesus Christ (Matthew 12:28).

3. The Word of God is used to cast out legions because it is like fire and a hammer (Jeremiah 23:29).

4. We cooperate with the Spirit of God or "the finger of God" to accomplish His will and purposes (Luke 11:20).

5

THE POWER OF GOD
IN PRAYER

*The imperative necessity of importunate prayer is
plainly set forth in the Word of God. It needs to be
stated and restated today. We are apt to overlook it
even more so today with all our comforts and ease. Yet,
it is a necessity for this surfeited age.*[4]

GOD BROUGHT SPIRIT-FILLED men into my life. It was a real
miracle after the life that I was used to and the upbringing
that I had, which were mostly negative. These godly men had
much experience with winning souls, counseling, and dealing
with the demonic or spirit world. As I listened to them, I
would go home and pray even more fervently. I had at least two
years without any influence from other people. I spent much
of my time in prayer and fasting. I really did not even know
who won the Super Bowl in those two years except when I
heard people talking about the games at church gatherings.

As I studied, fasted, and prayed, God began to challenge me to move in the direction of Africa. Some of my relatives were racists from the early 1960s. Imagine their response. I had been to a short-term mission trip in Guatemala. I wrestled with the thought of studying either Spanish or French. I thought to myself, What would they say if they knew God called me to go? Would they believe me? I always fell back on that God-inspired intuition about the leading of the Holy Spirit and call to Africa.

It was through my first short-term mission trip to Guatemala that God confirmed my calling to evangelism and missionary work. There in Guatemala, I saw a different people and their culture. I saw the difficulty of a life in poverty. I remember going to a church with experienced missionaries Dr. and Mrs. Sylwulka. The church was away from the comforts of the capital city.

What impacted me most was a man who walked to church several miles. He walked in the standard Guatemalan Indian dress. What was so amazing was that there was mud covering his sandals all the way up to his knees. He worshipped God without once washing. I shook his hand at the end of the service. I realized how committed he must have been to walk to church and sit unwashed through two hours of service.

In today's world, if you are not well-known or have an important name, it is difficult to receive the large amount of support needed to do mission enterprises. Unlike the early missionaries, many require a large budget. Many early missionaries took their clothes and shoes in one suitcase. They knew it was probable that they would be buried on foreign soil. All I knew is that God, not man, had called me to witness as I went (Matthew 20:18–20). It was equal to what He said to Abraham, "By faith Abraham, when he was called, obeyed by going out to a place, which he was to receive for an inheritance; and he went out, not knowing where he was going" (Hebrews 11:8). I prayed that intensely.

I always made appointments with God during those blessed days, spending hours on end on my knees. Prayer changes the Christian. In some mysterious way, God responds to prayer. It is not that we twist God's mind or make Him do something, which would be presumption, but that in the mystery, He accepts and answers our prayers. I began to pray fervently even though He could have said no. As I did so, I could see the reality of going to Africa coming closer over a period of eight years.

My wife worked days as a registered nurse at nursing facilities for the elderly. The company she worked for would move her from place to place as they needed. Her job was more like a substitute teacher. She made a definite impact on those she would take care of. She often had times of sharing the gospel. Many people, over the years, had commented how they wanted to send her to their job needs as she had the concern and mercy of Christ.

At the same time, I worked nights at a self-serve gasoline station. I would be busy with clients until 10:00 p.m., and then I would go to the back area and pray that God raise up the finances and prayer support to undergird the ministry to Africa. It took eight years for God to answer the request. Like Daniel, this request was held up by spiritual warfare:

> Then he said to me, "Do not be afraid, Daniel, for from the first day that you set your heart on this understanding this and on humbling yourself before your God, your words were heard, and I have come in response to your words. But the prince of the kingdom of Persia was withstanding me for twenty-one days; then behold, Michael, one of the chief princes came to help me, for I had been left there with the kings of Persia. Now I have come to give you an understanding of what will happen to your people in the latter day, for the vision pertains to the days yet future." (Daniel 10:12–14)

This was a time of testing and patience for both me and my wife. We could see that God did not answer our prayers very quickly as he did in Daniel's case of twenty-one days.

Our pastor said it would be good for preparation if we could live in the inner city. My wife and I moved there intentionally. We found a one-bedroom apartment with bars on the windows. It was during those times that thieves wanting the cash-register money at the easy store held me up. One thief came in, and I gave him the thirty-five dollars.

In those days, there was not a video camera or video surveillance. However, there was a twenty-dollar bill on the left side of the cash drawer. As I pulled it out to give it to the thief, a still camera took a photo of him. He never showed me his gun but held his right hand in the right-side pocket of his trench coat. He told me to give him the money, or there would be consequences.

I decided that if he told me to go lie down at the back, I was going to fight him. I was not going to let him shoot me without a struggle. However, all of a sudden, he said, "You are so calm and peaceful about all this." As I cooperated with him and gave him the money, he left the store with his thirty-five dollars. The police had me look at mug shots. After doing so, they found him, and he was arrested in about three days. There were two other instances like this while working there.

I can remember a man coming in the store with several friends. They took the cooked hot dogs, placed them in the buns, and put all the trimmings of condiments on them. I assumed they were going to pay and eat, but they threw them on the floor and then stomped them until they were ground up on top of the tile. They kept laughing about it and asking me what I was going to do to them. What could I do? They left, and I called the police. The police came about an hour later because they were so busy with crime.

I can remember once a gang of middle school students. There were about ten of them, and they came into the store daily. As they made their way through the store in a line, they would rapidly fill up their bags with candy or anything they could get their hands on. They did this for several weeks in a row. I came to find out that they were going from easy store to easy store within walking distance and terrorizing all the clerks. All the clerks called the police. As a consequence, they were caught and placed under the authority of the juvenile court.

Finally, I had the pizza and beer robber. He would come into the store each Friday night around 10:00 p.m. He would head straight to the cooler, pull out a frozen pizza and a six-pack of beer, and proceed to walk out with the goods. I called the police over several months, and they caught him.

Another night, two of us were working together. The company began to put two clerks in the store between 8:00 p.m. and 11:00 p.m. My coworker was from Iraq and a Moslem. That was not a coincidence. There was a snowy blizzard one night. A young woman came into the store and stole some headache medicine. My partner was fed up with her. The company had told us to let people have the money or the goods at any cost. Nevertheless, my coworker decided to run after the woman. He tracked her down at full speed, tackled her in the snow, removing her coat, and retrieved the medicine. She was out in the cold snow at night with her coat stripped off and without the medicine. During the time I worked at that convenience store, I shared the gospel with my partner and boss. Both were from Iraq and Moslems. It gave me preparation for our time to come in Africa. Praise be to God!

Remember, my wife and I lived in a three-room apartment. All the windows outside the apartment had bars on them. They were used to discourage thieves from breaking and entering. We had one of the apartments made from an old house. After living there a while, we noticed increased demonic activity. We could hear voices talking and doors would open and close. There were people walking outside our bedroom window all night long. They were talking about drugs and gangs. One evening, we both smelled something strange. Coming up through the floor of the bottom apartment was heavy smoke. I went outside and then down to the bottom apartment door. I knocked on the door. There was not a response. Therefore, I went in and saw two men lying on the kitchen floor. On the stove was a pot of chicken boiling. It had caught on fire. The stove was in flames. The apartment was loaded and overtaken with smoke. Meanwhile, my wife was calling the emergency line. I dragged both men out. They were passed out on the floor due to a heroin overdose. The firefighter came and put out the fire. They also administered oxygen to the two men out on the front lawn. They explained that had I not pulled them out, they would have died of smoke inhalation.

We told the owner we decided to move from the apartment. The next thing he told us was that a pastor had been murdered in the apartment we were renting. We moved to a different house about five blocks away.

At night, in the house we just had rented, our Sheltie dog named Lancer would often bark to warn us when someone was approaching our front street or porch. An elderly man lived in the carriage house behind us. As we heard this pounding on our front door, Lancer barked furiously. We asked at the door before opening it, "Who is it?" He said, "I am your neighbor from the back. Let me in. Someone has attacked me." We opened the door carefully, noticed it was our neighbor, and let him in. He was beaten up badly. The robbers had stolen his wallet with only five dollars in it. His head was bleeding, so my wife bandaged him up. He went home behind us in his carriage house rather shaken up.

In another event, our dog went barking furiously at the front door. Someone was banging on the door in a way that it sounded like a sledgehammer was being used. They kept shouting, "We know you have a hold for us." A *hold* is a cluster of drugs to sell. We yelled back through the closed door that the only *hold* we have is Jesus the Christ and locked the door. They left upon hearing the name of Jesus Christ.

I write all this to explain that prayer is essential in the Christian life. We faced so many "possibilities" of trouble every day during those times. Later, as I was in Northwest Africa, I would come to realize how God had pretrained me by prayer for the spiritual, emotional, and physical conflicts that would lie ahead. "Do you not see what it means to 'stand'? We do not try to gain ground; we merely stand on the ground which the Lord Jesus has gained for us, and resolutely refuse to be moved from it."[5]

We are so grateful to the prayer warriors who prayed faithfully for us regularly when we were in Africa. All our successes, protection, and the reason that we were not martyred are because of true born-again believers praying consistently for the ministry we were called to perform.

We can conclude as Andrew Murray wrote, "Prayerlessness is sin."[6] All ministries must be bathed in prayer, for the saints of old knew that to be the first essential ingredient to a successful Christian life and ministry. May God be glorified because of prayer.

Review: The Power of Prayer

1. Prayerlessness is sin (Matthew 6).[7]

   a. what a reproach it is to God

   b. the cause of a deficient spiritual life

   c. the dreadful loss that the church suffers as a result of the prayerlessness of the minister

   d. the impossibility of preaching the gospel to all men

2. Weapons of our warfare are not fleshly but mighty through God (2 Corinthians 10:3).

3. There is resistance to prayer in the spirit world (Daniel 10:12–14).

4. We stand in the strength that the Lord Jesus gives us against the spirit world (Ephesians 6:14).

In Summary

There is a power available to the church and the believer of this century that is untapped. The Church has presented to the world an inferior form of Christianity. Prayer is an essential ingredient in the life of a believer.[8]

6

THE FALSE CHRISTIAN MISSION IN THE UNITED STATES OF AMERICA

WHETHER WE AS the true church want to face the fact or not, there are deceivers within the church as a whole in the United States. They even start Christian missions and end up robbing the very missionaries and their churches they sign on. Their major concern for being involved in the enterprise is for *sordid gain*. They start out believing that their belief is true. They are so deceived they even think they are doing their mission for God, and so do other people. *Sordid* is a very strong word. According to the *Collegiate Dictionary*, it means "nasty; demonstrating the worst aspects of human nature such as immorality, selfishness, and greed; or squalid; dirty and nasty."[9] The apostle Paul faced the same type of opposition. In Titus 1:10–11, he writes (emphasis mine),

> For there are many rebellious men, empty talkers
> and deceivers, especially those of the circumcision,
> who must be silenced because they are upsetting
> whole families, teaching things they should not
> teach for the sake of *sordid gain*.

In addition, the apostle Peter warns other elders of the church to guard themselves against such hypocrisy when he writes in 1 Peter 5:2, "Shepherd the flock of God among you, exercising oversight not under compulsion, but voluntarily, according to the will God; and not for *sordid* gain, but with eagerness."

What's more, Satan intends to use these men and women to disrupt God's mission to the world. For some reason, God permits these people to continue in their folly. Some mission enterprises even use outside accountability resources. These Christian ministries are to investigate how independent missions use their money. They are supposed to be a financial watchdog. Quite frankly, it is very easy for mission enterprises to use people's money and hide it or place it in a different account, saying that the money is to be used for new projects. False prophets use a system of fraud to deceive the elect or people curious about the truth (Ezekiel 13:6–9, Jeremiah 29:9–32).

Take for instance a missionary we saw who would raise masses of money for his support. He stayed and lived in Northwest Africa deep into the bush. The extra money would be raised for special projects. With the money, he was to build huts or shelters or do other projects where he could hold Bible studies with seekers from Islam. The Bible study was to be shared around drinking tea, a common habit in that area of the world. He would build the projects and hold meetings, but without sharing the Bible with his Moslem friends. Come to find out most of the time, he was lying on the couch watching television. His monthly support at that time was about $5000 per month. Along with the project money, he had saved that cash and used it for worldly pursuits.

He and his wife recommended a Moslem doctor in the capital. Therefore, we took our child there to the Moslem doctor for examination. He told us he would write a receipt for $200, so when we were reimbursed by the insurance company, we would pay him $100 and keep $100 for ourselves. He said that is what the other missionary did. When we would not go along with it, he gave our child the wrong medicine and also overprescribed a medicine used to treat the condition I had when I saw him. The doctor gave me four times the dose, and because my wife was a nurse, she realized it was the wrong dose. I would have continued taking the medicine and could have died. This happened a few times, and then we realized that on the convincing of the other "missionary," this doctor really wanted to get us out of the way of the missionary's life. Eventually we went to another doctor trained in France.

At the time, I had several (very few) early morning Bible studies with this missionary. After about three meetings, he quit and said he was too busy while at the same time saying, "Get the word out." He would recommend his Moslem friends to do repairing of our cement walls inside our house. They would come in and intentionally throw cement in my shaving kit or medicine cabinet area. They performed a lousy and incomplete job so that we would be disappointed and displeased with them. It was a setup or railroad job. They were trying to force us to leave so he would not be caught, and the gospel was not shared.

We had African women who would help us around the house. One time, my wife caught this worker putting something into our water. We had a five-gallon water container that had filters in it called a Katadyn. The filters would kill or trap the bacteria so our water would be more or less bacteria-free. The helper was a friend of a missionary whom I will call the false brother missionary. For about six years after that time, the bottom of our feet would be so painful that we could barely walk on them. Even to this day, my wife at times will experience this pain. We believe we were poisoned. You must realize that if you turn to Christ in an Islamic world, it is likely that you will be poisoned. There are other missionaries who can document this fact.

When our son was about three years old, he played outside in the yard almost every day. One time, I saw him rounding the corner of a building only to see him step over a cobra without breaking stride. Fortunately, the cobra did nothing. It slithered away in normal fashion. My daughter and I were leaving a mission station out the front door when we were confronted by a cobra at full attention. I pushed my daughter back in the front door. The cobra went down to the ground only to rise up again at me and spread its hood. I hurriedly jumped inside, and then it slithered off. It's obvious that the angels of God were present.

I will never forget one of my best African friend's day of sorrow. He turned to Christ some forty years earlier as a Christian evangelist played music on the accordion and preached. He was from a Moslem home. He left that area and ended up in the capital city. He later had a family and children. The most sorrowful news was that his parents killed his son, their own grandson, by poisoning. In other words, the grandparents killed my friend's son because the son also turned to Christ. What a sorrowful way to lose a son. Persecution is expected in Islamic countries, whether moderate or radical. This persecution can be emotional by rejection; physical by means of poisoning, beating, and withholding food; or spiritual by the force of religious leaders' doctrine. Later on, he, another son, and his wife were beaten and stabbed by Moslem leaders.

It ended up that when we left North Africa, the mission enterprise was trying to leave us without the support we raised by our faithful prayer warriors and supporters. They prepared a setup. They wanted us to resign and have nothing to live on as we resettled in the United States. Fortunately, our pastor at the time stood up for us and demanded they pay us the support that we had so diligently raised through God's people. We came home from Africa with eight suitcases and some support and started all over, financially speaking. Those were rough times, but God saw us through. Through it all, we learned to trust in Jesus Christ even more.

The district attorney in the state they were stationed said we should bring it before the courts and expose them. We decided we did not want the attention the media would have given to the situation. A well-meaning lawyer and the prosecutors of the state said we could be invited to share our story on *60 Minutes*.

Did not Jesus Christ teach fellow Christians to *love one another*? It was obvious to us that this missionary and their leaders were not real Christians but ran the ministry for *sordid* gain. The whole point of this chapter is to describe that evil impostors do exist as the first apostles experienced. Moreover, in the modern world we live in, it still exists. Most of the time, we think of those robbing the church on television programs. However, imagine impostors using Christian mission as the backbone of their deception and theft. In addition, as we might think denominations are not free from this, how do we know that these whom we trust are actually using the money as we think they are? We do not always know. This is no excuse for not giving. We give on the basis of faith. The good news is once someone gives money to a ministry, that person is not accountable for what the ministry does with it. The minister or ministry will give an account to God one day. Therefore, there is not an excuse for not giving. "For such men are false apostles, deceitful workers, disguising themselves as apostles of Christ. No wonder, for even Satan disguises himself as an angel of light" (2 Corinthians 11:13–16).

Review: The False Christian Mission in the United States of America

1. There will always be impostors who use religion to gain money (Titus 1:16).

2. Apostates are those who renounce a belief or an allegiance to a cause. The Bible is replete of examples of this type of ungodly people (2 Thessalonians 2:3).

3. Islam is a religion that forces its people to believe by intimidation. In Islam, there is not a concept of love. Allah only loves his believers when they love him. True *agape* love is a moral attribute of the true and living God. Islam threatens those who are disobedient with pressure, fear, and coercion—and even death threats. With Islam, there is no need for a sacrifice for the sin problem. There is never assurance of salvation nor assurance of eternal life (1 John 5:10–13).

7

ISLAM AND EVANGELISM

ONE OF THE first doctrines of Islam is, in essence, Allah is unique and has no son.[10]

Islam attacks the very nature of the gospel by attacking the legitimacy of Jesus Christ as the Son of God, the Christ, the Messiah, our God, and the only sacrifice for sins. It is also a dominant religion in the 10/40 Window, as are the religions of Hinduism and Buddhism. The 10/40 Window is a window that missiologists have designated as the largest area of unreached people groups in the world. It reaches from the most western point of West Africa to the most eastern point of China. It extends from ten degrees to forty degrees north of the equator. It contains the largest populations of non-Bible-believing Christians in the world. Islam is trying to destroy the United States of America. At the time of this writing, the leaders of our country claim to be wise. What they cannot see is that Satan is using Islam in our country to destroy it. We must call all Christians to stand firm against this evil doctrine of religion. Christians must hate the doctrines of Islam but love the Moslems.

You must consider the cost if you are going to go share the gospel in front-line territory with Moslem people. Satan has ordered his principalities, powers, rulers, and wicked spirits to resist persistently the preaching of the gospel in many of these areas of the world. It was no different where we worked. There was often a sense of heaviness or an oppressive intuition that made many workers feel like giving up. On the other hand, at times, the Holy Ghost was so powerful that we were of the opinion we were ready to "fly" into heaven and meet Jesus Christ immediately. The result would be that our testifying became easy and comfortable even if we were threatened. We heard about the tragic cost paid by others who were ministering in the same area of the world. They had their lives ended early.

We would often go far out into the bush where the gospel had never before been shared. Periodically, the African children would come up to us, grabbing our hands or touching our skin. This was because they had never before seen white people. Sometimes they would offer us fresh goat's milk and then apologize that they had nothing more to offer us. We drank it gratefully. The important key was that they had been indoctrinated with the prophet Muhammad but had never heard the name of Jesus Christ. We would always share the gospel. As we left, they would sometimes say, "You are a true prophet from God because we have never heard such a message." There were areas deep into the bush that could only be traversed during the dry season. When the rainy season came, the people were landlocked until the water subsided many months later. Some of them would die if they ran out of supplies because of the high water. Because of the inability to travel, malaria took the lives of many, especially children, in this area of North Africa.

Photo with African children

Several missionaries were driving in from deep in the bush to go to a meeting in the capital city. The Christian driver of the vehicle fell asleep, and if I remember correctly, four missionaries were killed. You must understand that out there deep into the land, there are no telephones and not a single 911 respondent, no police, and there is not any emergency equipment. If you have an accident, you are totally in the hands and trust of Almighty God. There was another instance where a mother was watching her two-year-old out in the yard. She went to do something for about thirty seconds and came back to find her son had drowned in a five-gallon bucket of water, leaving her only to bury him right away. Another missionary couple lost their young son to leukemia. In only several hours, he passed away without little medication or hospital treatment.

I remember a time when we were in our car in the capital city. Many in the city were on strike because they were angry about the politics of the country and the bus system. We were making shopping rounds at the market when, all of a sudden, we saw about one hundred citizens stoning a bus loaded with people. We turned around quickly, jumping up a curb and island, so that we could escape the vicious attack.

We used to go to the capital city every three months or so to receive our support money and to get out of the extreme heat. We would experience temperatures where we worked anywhere from 90 degrees at dawn to 130 degrees at three o'clock in the afternoon. We would spend about ten days in the capital and then head out again to the place where God had called us to work. We usually drove in at night because we did not have air conditioning in our first vehicle.

One time, while we were driving, we hit a camel on the road. Thanks to our Heavenly Father's protection, we escaped harm. As I hit the camel, it rolled onto the car hood. My wife held on to our young son, still an infant, and we assumed the camel would crash into the windshield. We thought we would all die or be severely hurt. Angels of God pushed the camel off the car. The only evidence of the accident was camel hair stuck to the license plate and to the windshield washer blades and a small dent in the hood. It is proof that those who believe have angels ministering to them. "And of the Angels He says, Who makes His angels winds, And His ministers a flame of fire" (Hebrews 1:7).

It is not an easy task to work as a Christian evangelist in the area of North Africa. Most likely, you would be stoned if you presented yourself as a Christian missionary preaching the gospel in Mauritania. There is real, hard evidence of this happening. Because I was an American evangelist, I would never cross the river into Mauritania. I knew I would be taking a great risk of losing my life, and my children would grow up without a father. Yes, even our children were at risk daily of being poisoned or exposed to other dangers. I can recall my wife going to our Moslem neighbors and found our son playing with a butcher knife. The neighbors had let their children play with it. My wife brought our son home after seeing him with the knife. When she questioned why they let their children play with such a sharp object, their answer was, "Oh well, only God knows"—the famous Islamic line of fatalism.

I can remember the day that my associate, an African evangelist from another African country, and another friend who was not a Christian crossed the river into Mauritania. They both returned scared to death but content to be alive. They had approached a village directly on the other side of the river from our town to share the gospel with them. It did not last long. The chief called out the whole village. They picked up stones and threatened them to leave or be stoned.

Even though we were in a "moderate" Islamic country, there were always threats from the marabout. A marabout is a leader in the Moslem faith, one who would be called a saint. They control the people by threatening them or withholding food or support from them. Although you would expect them to be a real threat to us, God often protected us by sending angels to encamp around us.

The Moslem man we rented from had placed a voodoo doll up in our ceiling. Over the course of a few years, he would ask us if everything was going all right. We did not know the voodoo doll was placed there. He trusted in his Islam and the spirit world to get rid of us. Often Moslems would wear *gris-gris*, a term for an item used in witchcraft that is worn as a bracelet or around the neck to ward off evil spirits. They are also used to bring curses on others. I am convinced that was attempted on our family very often. My wife would get up at night with our young son, who was often ill with ear infections. Each night, she saw a "wicked spirit" manifest by walking through the front door and leaving by the back door. It was a dark figure with a long robe and hood.

For ten days during our missionary stay, we had a group from the Unites States come and visit our field of service. We warned the group about the manifestation of the spirit. The spirit manifested, and two men from the group saw it. One of them was surprised but aware of the spirit world. The other man was in shock, and we never heard from him again after his return to the United States.

I had shared the gospel in Bambara through cassette tapes with two men from the next country. Bambara is a trade language found in parts of West Africa. I played the recording on tape of 1 John. The two men agreed that it was the truth and wanted to receive Jesus Christ as Savior and Lord. I explained to them that they should renounce spiritism, burn their gris-gris, renounce the satanic world, and believe in the Lord Jesus Christ. They did and prayed with me to receive Christ. Alexander the Coppersmith was angry that I challenged them to give up all for Jesus Christ.

There were days when God's mighty power was at work. One time, I drove around a medium-sized town with about six to ten thousand inhabitants in the area. I told them by word of mouth that we would be showing *The Jesus Film* from Campus Crusade for Christ that evening. It was in their language. I expected a decent turnout, but God did a miracle by allowing about 1,500 people there to see it. They sat down in the desert dust. This was in the desert where the dirt was something like what you would have in your vacuum cleaner. We showed the film in the evenings. Because that area of the world was mosquito-infested, I can remember being sick with malaria that night but well enough to share the gospel film. We really do not know the impact as the film itself asks for a decision to believe. I followed up with people afterward and found it was the women who probably made decisions for Christ. Of course, they would be unable to publicly confess Christ immediately for several reasons. One, it was polygamy, and they would risk being ejected from their camp. Two, it was likely they would be beaten by their husband or beaten up by the other wives.

Again, at another time, we drove out to a far-off village wanting to share *The Jesus Film*. The leader-chief of the village talked for ten minutes about showing *The Jesus Film*. He said he would get back to us with his decision. We waited for over an hour. His decision was that we could show the film, but not in the town. We would have to go to an area by the school. This was late, after dark, and most Africans were finishing the late evening meal. The school was about a mile away. There we set up the screen and movie projector. Despite the leaders warning the people against it, over one hundred people came to see the film. They also sat down in the desert dust for the entire length of the film.

The African evangelist and I saw several instances of demonic possession. The first one was a young boy shackled on a long chain about thirty feet long. He was attached to an old run -down mud house; inside, there was shelter from the elements. We asked his father if he wanted us to minister to the young man. He said no, so we left the area, watching the son scream out as is described in Mark chapter 5. The second was evidenced when we tried to share the gospel with an elderly woman in the courtyard outside her house. We made the usual several minutes of greetings and asked if we could sit down and share some good news with her. She said yes. After we introduced ourselves, we began sharing the gospel message. As soon as we spoke a few sentences, a sheep would act wildly and run in circles around the mud house and baa like nothing I have ever seen. It knocked over pots and pans violently. Although very distracting, the sheep settled down, and we began to share the gospel again. Each time we began to share, it would repeat the same action. The woman locked it up into a makeshift pen. It continued to baa madly, but we were able to share the good news of the gospel with her.

In another instance, we went to share the gospel with a young man who claimed to have magical powers associated with Islam. His one-room mud house was infested with mice. He lived in extreme poverty. As we sat down to talk with him, many mice scurried out along from under his sheets and bedcovers. He started talking about the spirit world and asked us if we wanted him to call up a sheep. The sheep would be brought up from the spirit world at his command. What he wanted to do was to call on the spirit world to manifest an entity, a fallen angel, fashioned like a sheep. We told him yes, that would be fine, but first we would pray in the name of Jesus Christ. He continued telling us of his magical powers but did not call up the sheep because of his refusal for us to pray in the name of Jesus Christ. The key of the discussion was the name *Jesus*

Christ. I believe that he was unable to perform his sorcery because of the name above all names, *Jesus Christ.*

The marabout would send children to throw rocks at our gate. We lived in a mud house with a tin roof. We had concrete block walls and a steel gate to keep people out when they were not invited. If you do not have defense, some Africans will come night and day into your camp and even march directly into your bedroom. Therefore, the gate was kept closed for many of the hours after 9:00 p.m. The marabout would also send children to harass us by chanting. They would do this by climbing the tree that overlooked our house then throw rocks and chant, "Kris Christian."

During our time there, our children were not immune to sicknesses and assaults. Our daughter had friends she played with daily. One time, one of her friends named Bitsy was angry with us. We think her family was telling her about us Christians and not to believe the gospel. We had a regular Bible study every Wednesday afternoon, and our guitarist played simple Christian songs. I used photo cards to show stories from the gospel, such as Jesus walking on water. We gave out candy or little cookies at the end of the study, and Bitsy's family had been angry. Come to find out, Bitsy poured hot tea directly onto our daughter's ankle. Her ankle was scarred from that point on. We had shared the gospel with Bitsy's mother several times, only two weeks before she collapsed from a heart attack.

In another instance, my wife was visiting a camp in the evening with our two-year-old who son, who was walking around the camp. The common practice was to set up a campfire to give light and to cook the evening meal. The fire was made from wood found deep into the bush. People would use a donkey and cart to load up wood and bring it in to sell. The evening meal was usually eaten after dark. All of a sudden, our son fell on his side directly on top of the fire, where a pot of tea was cooking. My wife jumped up to pull him off the fire, and to our surprise, he was not burned at all. Even the Africans in the camp were astonished that he did not have one single burn. The angels of God had protected him completely from harm.

There were few motorcycles in the area where we worked. One sped by in front of our house, where our son was outside with my wife. The motorcycle came inches away from hitting him, and by a miracle, he was never hit. Our son had been sick with ear infections throughout the time of our early ministry there, and one night he was very ill. We believed that he had pneumonia and used a nebulizer to help open his lungs so he could breathe. He was gasping for air, and his face had a strange color, but he was not yet blue. My wife finally gave him Pediazole, which supporting doctors had given us to bring with us from the United States. After we gave him the medicine, he started to recover. We were then able to drive the twelve hours to the capital city and see a trained medical physician from France.

Our success in evangelizing came through personal relationships. We met Otis Dee and Mim See. After many months of befriending them and sharing with them our common bond as neighbors, we shared the gospel with them many times. They named their newborn daughter after my wife, Nancy. This is a sign, against the counsel of the marabout, that they were close to understanding the gospel. We left with them a hand cassette player so they could play tapes of the gospel message in their language without electricity or batteries.

Oftentimes we ministered to Moslems by taking them to the market, taking women in childbirth to a midwife, and used our car as a funeral hearse. In one instance, I took a young woman about twenty-five years old and her young child to the medical clinic that was about twelve miles away. She had the child wrapped in a piece of tissue called a turban. By the time we arrived at the medical clinic, the child had died. We returned to our village only to let the mother off to bury her child. We agreed to pay for the funeral cloth worth about ten dollars. The average salary was only about one dollar per day in that country.

The medical clinic was a simple block building with each room having a separate door, and it was more like a small bedroom. Sick people would come and lie in front of the door waiting to get a "bed." These were old beds with their springs broken and mattresses used for years and years, probably from World War II. There were no cleaning products available. You can imagine the stench as deathly ill people lay there in desperation of help. Some were already dead, waiting to be taken off and buried in the desert sand. There was only one trained medical doctor, an African trained in France. Suffering and death were a common part of their daily life.

Other neighbors named their son after me. Little *Kris* was born physically and mentally handicapped. The woman named Mimi gave him to us to take care of. We nurtured and took care of him until he died at the age of one year from heart complications. Through that ministry, the family always defended us from harm against other radical Moslems.

Review: Islam and Evangelism

1. Doctrines of the Quran concerning Jesus Christ are
    blasphemous (see *The Meaning of The Holy Quran*,
    English version).

2. Moslems sometimes use witchcraft to try to harm
    Christian workers and their own people. This is
    called *syncretism* or the combining of religious
    beliefs. Some Moslems use witchcraft to harm
    and to curse their own people. Again, syncretism, a
    combination of different beliefs, is used to harm or
    dismay people. Using force and the threat of curses
    is part of their everyday lifestyle.

3. Developing personal relationships with Moslems is
    essential in winning them to Christ. They must see
    that you love (*agape*) them.

8

FALSE APOSTLES, PROPHETS, AND DECEITFUL WORKERS

As BORN-AGAIN BELIEVERS, we are convinced that Islam is a man-made religion or, should I say, a doctrine of the fallen angel Lucifer, according to my interpretation of Muhammad's testimony. We took note that God did not speak directly to Muhammad, but an angel did speak to him. The revelation to Muhammad was this:

> And now, behold! A dazzling vision of beauty and light overpowered his senses, And he heard the word "Iqra!" "Iqra!" which being interpreted may mean "Read!" "Proclaim!" or "Recite!" The unlettered Prophet was puzzled; He could not read. The Angel seemed to press him to his breast in a close embrace, And the cry rang clear "Iqra!"[11]

Islam attacks the doctrine of the Bible on the person and work of Jesus Christ. The Quran states that they do blaspheme who say that Jesus is God.

> Of Allah aught but the truth. Christ Jesus the son of Mary Was (no more than) A Messenger of Allah, And His Word, Which He bestowed on Mary, And a Spirit proceeding From Him: so believe In Allah and His Messengers. Say not "Trinity": desist.[12]

Islam equates saying Christ as a Begotten Son no more than blasphemy, and since Allah cannot have intercourse, Jesus is no more than a doctrine of an animal act associated with paganism.[13] Islam claims that the Quran is a new revelation from God. The scriptures of the Bible were brought to us from God to man by man, not by an angel to man by man. This is why the Quran cannot be a new revelation from God following the Bible. The Quran contradicts itself when it says in Surah 3:3, "It is He Who sent down To thee (step by step), In truth, the Book, Confirming what went before it; And He sent down the law (Of Moses) and the Gospel (of Jesus)."[14]

It is the same way with Roman Catholicism. The Roman Catholic church has not always been as it is today. The beginning of the exaltation of Mary (the mother of Jesus) and the term *Mother of God* was first applied to her by the Council of Ephesus in 431 AD. In the Bible, there is not any mention of Mary, the mother of Jesus, as a person to be worshipped or consulted through imagery or prayer. This would be contrary to the first of the Ten Commandments in Exodus 20:3 and Deuteronomy 18:9–20.

Apostle Paul makes the truth clear to us in Galatians 1:8: "But even if we, or an angel of heaven, should preach to you a gospel contrary to what we have preached to you, he is to be accursed." Make no bones about it. There are false apostles, false prophets, and false Christians in the world today. We recognize them by Paul's statement. Oftentimes we fail to acknowledge that there are false Christians on the inside, or in the parachurch, stealing money and making the lives of true believers a nightmare. However, Apostle Paul was very aware of this and wrestled with it often.

Should not we be quick to recognize that part of our problem as Christians in the United States is that some ministries are false? In order to make that well-known, those who know about them would have to come out and stand together in prayer against the forces of evil behind them. It is true that the church within the United States is *Laodicean* in nature in many areas. After all, if it is true that there are far more than one hundred thousand church buildings in the USA, then why does revival tarry, and why do we sense that our country is terribly out of order? Many ministers believe it is a serious spiritual problem of our times. We complain about it, but the evangelistic life of the average churchgoer is pitiful. We do not have the fervency that Paul wrote about in 2 Timothy 1: 7: "For God has not given us a spirit of timidity, but of power and love and discipline."

Preachers are afraid to preach the cross of Christ because they might lose their salaries. The apostle Paul had everything to lose, and he did, but that did not stop him from preaching the cross (1 Corinthians 1:18). Christians are afraid to testify because they might lose their jobs. Many Christians do not want to be known as notorious. Not one Christian wants to suffer through being accused falsely. That is exactly what is happening to those who share the gospel in many parts of the world, especially among Moslems. God may be in the process of thinning the ranks in these United States, or it may be that He is getting ready to expose us and blow winds of revival here by His mighty power.

Do we not recognize the words of Jesus when he said, "Do not think I came to bring peace on the earth; I did not come to bring peace, but a sword" (Matthew 10:34). The gospel divides families and friends. Nevertheless, to take it a step further, the gospel teaching should identify false and true Christians for us so that we are not deceived.

Apostle is from a Greek word in the New Testament *apostolos*, which means "one who is sent by God as a messenger, a commissioner of Christ, with miraculous power; and an ambassador of the gospel; and one who represents the name or authority of the person that he speaks for."[15] *Ambassador* and *missionary* are similar ideas but also different. Our modern word *missionary* does not relate exactly what is meant in scripture. However, they are all "sent forth."

> As a spiritual gift, the gift of apostle would be defined as: the ability and responsibility to be sent by Jesus Christ to communicate His Gospel and establish His Church, especially where it has not been before.[16]

Many times, believers think that it is the church, or rules of a denomination, that sends forth workers. It is not the church who appoints; it is God. "A missionary is not always sent of God. Sometimes a denomination sends them out."[17] Workers, sent ones, have to be chosen and sent by God. I have seen so-called missionaries on the mission field, missionaries who never shared *the* faith, nor did they talk about Christ crucified.

Paul states, "Through whom we have received grace and *apostleship* to bring about the obedience of faith among all the Gentiles for His name's sake" (Romans 1:5). A true apostle or "sent one" shares the gospel so that when someone becomes a Christian, they will obey *the faith*. This includes all that is in the gospel message—of salvation from sin and to victory in Christ Jesus and eternal life. "The Faith which was once for all handed down to the Saints" (Jude 3).

Paul also warns us that there are *false apostles* or *false sent ones* and *false* missionaries. This may include people in bogus church organizations, artificial mission boards, and counterfeit parachurch ministries, and false Christians in denominations. Paul warns us of this idea (emphasis mine):

> For such men are false apostles, *deceitful workers*, disguising themselves as apostles of Christ. No wonder, for even Satan disguises himself as an angel of light. (2 Corinthians 11:13–15)

> I know your deeds and your toil and perseverance, and that you cannot tolerate *evil men*, and you put to the test all those who call themselves *apostles*, and they are not, and you found them to be *false*; and you have perseverance and have endured for my names sake, and have not grown weary. (Revelation 2:2)

This is true especially in these days as we head toward the rapture and the tribulation.

> For they are *spirits of demons*, performing signs which go out to the kings of the whole world, to gather them together for the war of that great day of God, the Almighty. (Revelation 16:14)

Those people and ministries are what Jesus calls "tares" in Matthew 13:25. A tare is any of several weedy plants that grow in grainfields, and an unwelcome or objectionable element.[18] Those who operate in ministry as tares, as sent ones, are repugnant to God.

A self-proclaimed prophetess influenced the early church into sexual immorality. Her name was Jezebel. The spirit of Jezebel represents paganism. The deeds of the Nicolaitans reflect the same concept of immorality influencing the church (Revelation 2:6, 20). Ahab's wife, Jezebel, influenced Old Testament Jews into idolatry and immorality (1 Kings 16:31–33). Americans accept immorality as a normal part of the culture, and it is becoming rampant among our young people. The church has not explained well the concept of sacred marriage and the holiness of the relationship between a man and a woman.

Jesus Christ said, "Beware of false prophets, who come to you in sheep's clothing, but inwardly are ravenous wolves" (Matthew 7:15). The whole concept of ravenous wolves is that they do not care who they hurt, kill, or destroy as long as they get what they want. It is usually money received by *sordid gain*.

> In all things show yourself to be an example of good deeds, with purity in doctrine dignified, sound in speech which is beyond reproach, so that the opponent will be put to shame, having nothing bad to say about us. (Titus 2:7)

Review: False Apostles, Prophets and Deceitful Workers

1. The gospel is called the glad tidings or good news.
    Religion may make a person feel good, but it cannot
    satisfy the longing of being in a personal relationship
    with God through the Lord Jesus Christ. In the case
    of Islam, "Allah" is not a personal God but only a
    judge without love, unless you love Allah first.
    Doctrines in Islam say that "Allah" allows grace and
    mercy, but there is not any indication of a personal
    aspect of him in the Quran that would guarantee
    assurance of salvation or eternal life for anyone,
    not even for a faithful Moslem, except for killing
    and suicide.

    Roman Catholicism fails to recognize both the
    revelation of Jesus Christ in the biblical scriptures
    and the illumination of those same scriptures in
    a personal way to true believers. It is hard for a
    Protestant to understand the fear that a priest has
    over his parishioners. The Roman Catholic Church
    puts the priest between a follower and the knowledge
    of God as revealed in the scriptures as it relates to
    forgiveness of sins. This makes the priest the sole
    interpreter of truth. It puts the priest between the
    confession of sins and the forgiveness of sins. Jesus
    Christ alone is our High Priest (Hebrews 3:1). This
    is the obvious fallacy of false workers who hold the

fear of one's eternal destiny over them, acting as if they are God (Isaiah 52:5–7).

2. True missionaries or "sent ones" are God-called, Godsent, and God-empowered. Groups of believers can confirm this calling. They often use the term *appointees* as newly sent missionaries. The church in times past and present has tried to "control" those who are called by God by excluding certain converts. It is our opinion that faith missionaries live out of an accepted standard comfort zone because of their calling. They require total dependency on God to provide resources to live and accomplish the work of the ministry (Galatians 1:11–17).

3. There will always be evil, deceitful workers, tares, and those who steal money within the connection of the true church. They have denied godliness, and we are to avoid them (2 Timothy 3:1–9).

4. False workers and false religions are troubled by spirits of demons (demonic forces) and cooperate with them for self-gain and power, often without knowing it (1 Timothy 4:1).

5. True workers are known by their doing of good to other members of the body of Christ as a result of sowing to the Spirit (Galatians 6:7–10).

9

ALEXANDER, DEMAS, AND FRIENDS

JESUS CHRIST SAID, "Blessed are those who have been persecuted for the sake of righteousness, for theirs is the Kingdom of heaven. Blessed are you when people insult you and persecute you, and falsely say all kinds of evil against you because of Me" (Matthew 5:10–11).

While in Africa, we finally had some success with the Moslems. Many were admitting, mostly privately due to fear, that Islam held no future for them. The power structure was being influenced, and people were questioning where they would spend eternity. As never before, the preaching of biblical Christianity, the eternal gospel, through the power of the Holy Spirit was exposing this around the region where we worked. The Holy Spirit was also exposing the unfruitful works of the darkness of Islam. We were well-known in faraway villages even though we had never gone to them.

This made a serious dilemma for Islamic leaders. They believe in Jesus as a prophet. There was a private turbulence by the leaders to do away with us. Therefore, instead of killing us outright, a conspiracy was developed. The missionary, whom I will address as Alexander the Coppersmith, and the mission I wrote about in chapter 6 went to work. "Alexander the Coppersmith did me much harm; the Lord will repay him according to his deeds. Be on guard against him yourself. For he vigorously opposed our teaching" (2 Timothy 4:14).

We were wondering what was going on because we found that our daughter's cat had been poisoned and died. Two of our children were playing on a mound of sand that construction workers were going to mix with cement for masonry and building purposes. Alexander drove along in his four-by-four truck and started to climb up on it as if he were going to run over them. Just at that moment, one of Alexander's associates saw him doing it. He told me that as he was climbing the sandpile, the wheels were spinning so close to my children, and he was laughing about it the whole time. It was obvious at that point that a hatred and jealousy had developed in Alexander against my family.

Alexander and his leaders, upon pressure from Moslems, arranged a meeting so we did not have a defense. We asked for a mediator to be present at the meeting so it would not be one-sided, but that was not allowed. This is so typical of cults and false Christians because they never allow a fair hearing between two parties. It was the most hideous meeting I have ever attended. My wife and I were attacked and abused emotionally almost to the point of brainwashing. Many counselors call the result of this tactic post-traumatic stress syndrome. They kept chanting one after the other that we were rotten people. They even said they did not believe that God forgives our sin as far as the east is from the west (Psalm 103:12).

Fortunately, we were not damaged emotionally to the point of that stress syndrome. The whole plan of all cults and false ministries follows these things. First, they attempt to make their victims have a thorough psychological breakdown; and second, they use reeducation to control their victims. These two things fulfill their own need for power and control. This control is usually financial *sordid gain* or sexual (in the case of Islam), and the end result is indoctrination. We can relate this to a religious cult operated by Jim Jones, the founder and leader of the Peoples Temple. His cult took place in Jonestown, Guyana. I believe the reason we were not damaged is that we had an awesome prayer support group who prayed for us regularly, and we understood from training how to resist the demonic spiritual world and spiritual warfare. We also had trust in God, which kept our mind renewed and our hearts set toward the true and living God. This confirms the truth that Satan's kingdom will use anyone it will, either through nonbelievers or even through believers. We thank God for His grace on our lives, or we would not be here today.

Alexander the Coppersmith even convinced my friend to go along with him so he could receive money to go to the United States. I will address him as Demas. "For Demas, having loved this present world, has deserted me and gone to Thessalonica" (2 Timothy 4:10). Demas was an African from another African country. He told us that in his country, when food or money was low, his family would skin, cook, and eat domesticated cats. I met him in the capital city. He claimed to be a Christian but told me he could not put the novels he was reading away. It was obvious that the spirit world had control of him, and he often complained of nightmares. I talked to him about the Son of God, Jesus Christ, and prayed with him. Over a period of a few weeks, he was reading his Bible. It was somewhere along that point that he confessed Christ Jesus publicly among many missionaries in the capital city. Later, he was baptized in the river that separates the country we worked in from Mauritania. In this case, his testimony revealed a turning away from the truth as Demas had Paul the apostle.

Before the time of our being forced out of ministry, he became good friends with Alexander the Coppersmith. It was so obvious that they developed a conspiracy because I would share plans of ministry with him, and later, I would find out that he reported these things to Alexander to be used against us. He even did something to our movie projector so that we could not show *The Jesus Film*. *The Jesus Film* is a film about the Gospel of Luke. I had the only key to a spare room in the house that we lived in. Demas knew where that key was placed and used it when we were gone from the house to disengage part of the movie projector. I had to call the leader from Campus Crusade for Christ to guide me on how to put the projector back in working order. The goal of Demas, on the persuasion of Alexander the Coppersmith, was to prevent the showing of *The Jesus Film*. This was on orders of Alexander and the conspiracy they developed. I had written permission from Moslems in the town we lived in to show this *Jesus* film. I took all the proper steps to get the showing approved so that the Moslems would not say we showed it without their permission.

This false mission sent two spies out to work with us and work on us. One was there to help us settle in and to do odd jobs, like painting, to be involved in ministry. In the meantime, he was recording many things we said. We came to find out that he put a microphone in our room and recorded private discussions between my wife and me. He also asked me questions concerning our mission pastor at the sending church. I only told him that he would usually mention other ministries than ours and would talk about money appropriated for other ministries. A good friend of ours knew of a Christian in a congregation who gave seven thousand dollars to our work. However, those seven thousand dollars were not proportioned to our mission work until I questioned the mission minister about it.

The purpose of the three-day meeting was to discredit us with our supporters and churches and to send us back to the United States. We had young children at the time, and their lives were on the line as well. Alexander, Demas, and their friends accomplished their goal. We felt threatened physically. I decided to get my family out. Early one morning, we packed up essential things and drove the fourteen hours back to the capital city, and my family got out of the country. Finally, I was forced to get my family out of the area. We packed up our things and left during the night. Somehow the trailer hitch ball was loose. We were about two hours from the capital when the trailer fell off the hitch. It rolled several times, almost killing bystanders waiting for a car of transport to take them farther into the bush. I looked back in my rearview mirror, and there wasn't any way we could continue driving at a normal speed in the difficult dirt road. Some Africans helped me turn the trailer right side up. I wrapped the safety chains around the hitch area where the ball was loose. I was able to proceed about five miles per hour. At that rate, we would arrive in the capital city in about sixteen more hours. Then all of a sudden, there was a miracle. I looked to the right of our vehicle while driving. There were a group of workers welding. They were working on pipes for a deep water well. This was absolutely in the outer bush in the uttermost parts of the world. There wasn't any village or villagers around. It was basically desolate of any human interaction. So I went to the welders and asked them if they would weld the ball back on the hitch. They gladly welded it. What a miracle! We were able to continue our journey all the way back to the capital city. My family left for the United States, and I did not know if I would see them again.

Alexander was behind the scene, approving all this. I decided to leave everything that was usable in the town where we lived in instead of moving it, selling it, or giving them away in the capital city. Some of the things were bought. While I was closing down the ministry, about seventy-five Moslems lined up sitting on the walls outside our house, and they would not leave.

They were there to threaten me. Although Demas was with me, I could tell he was not with me, if you know what I mean. Early one morning, the day I was to leave for the capital, a Moslem I will call Yayaaha (with whom I had shared the gospel many times) put a butcher knife to my back around the area of my kidneys. He wanted to thrust it into my lower back and kill me. However, for some strange reason, he did not do it. He could have gotten away with killing me. The Holy Spirit brought to my remembrance during this time, "Do not fear those who kill the body but are unable to kill the soul; but rather fear Him who is able to destroy both soul and body in hell" (Matthew 10:28). He would have claimed many false accusations against me, and many well-meaning Christians may have even believed him. Many Christians in the United States have never faced such opposition or death threats, so it seems far-fetched to believe this type of persecution really happens to us as American Christians.

Back in the United States, the false mission told our church that we should come home. They wanted the money that we had raised. Sordid gain, revenge, and hate were all part of their scheme. Christian people had donated for a car so that we could travel and evangelize the large desert area we lived in. They believed if we left the mission, they would receive the sum from those donations and leave us without money to live on in the United States. It backfired! They did not get what they thought they would, and in fact, our pastor at the time helped us reestablish in the United States. Glory be to God! A definition of a pastor is someone who shepherds his flock, and this includes protecting them from false Christians.

Well-meaning church leaders in the USA tried to counsel us through this situation. It was hard for them to believe that a large parachurch organization operated like the Mafia. One attorney suggested we just leave this alone because they were deranged people. Accordingly, on our return to the United States, the leaders questioned us. To our disbelief, they did not believe us right away, and many to this day never understood what happened to us. They turned away from us, as Paul experienced with Phygelus and Hermogenes (2 Timothy 1:15).

Similarly, Alexander forced another missionary family, the associate the he used to make us leave, to leave the foreign field. Nine months after our removal, Alexander purged them from his presence. One in the family ended up in a psychiatric unit for six months. Isaiah commented on Israel's false prophets and irresponsible leaders in this way:

> His watchman are blind, all of them know nothing. All of them are mute dogs unable to bark, dreamers lying down. Who love to slumber; and the dogs are greedy, they are not satisfied. And they are shepherds who have no understanding; They have all turned toward their own way, each one to his unjust gain, to the last one. (Isaiah 56:10–11)

The apostle Peter warned us to be aware of false teachers and unbelievers. "Know this first of all, that in the last days mockers will come with their mocking, following after their own lusts." (2 Peter 3:3).

An answer to our circumstance came mightily by the power of the Holy Spirit. It was 1 Peter 4:12–13:

> Beloved, do not be surprised at the fiery ordeal among you, which comes upon you for your testing, as though some strange thing were happening to you; but the degree that you share the sufferings of Christ, keep on rejoicing, so that also the revelation of his glory you may rejoice with exaltation.

No matter the circumstance, we must obey God even if *nobody* supports us. Paul says, "At my first defense no one supported me, but all deserted me; may it not be counted against them" (2 Timothy 4:16).

Review: Alexander, Demas, and Friends

1. The immoral person in 1 Corinthians 5:5 was handed over to Satan, and so were Hymenaeus and Alexander the Coppersmith because they would not repent (1 Corinthians 5:5, 1 Timothy 1:20).

2. Deceivers and nonbelievers trust in idols, especially money (Psalm 135:15).

3. False workers do not want to be persecuted for the cross of Christ (Galatians 6:12).

4. Justice will be completed in due time (Matthew 10:26).

5. No person or spiritual entity can hide from God or El Roi (Psalm 10:11, Hebrews 4:13).

6. We recognize true believers because they refrain from practicing sin as a habit of life (2 Timothy 2:19, 1 John 3:9–10).

7. Forgiveness of people who try to hurt us is an important key to triumphant Christian living, and applying that forgiveness defeats wicked spiritual entities. Forgiveness is a choice, not a feeling (2 Timothy 4:16–18, Matthew 18:21–35).

10

DECEITFUL SPIRITS AND DOCTRINES OF DEMONS

THE SIGNS OF the times indicate to us as Christians that impostors within our lines will fall away from the faith. We usually attribute this to original sin or personal choices of sin. If we look at the overall grand scheme of things, we see that the scriptures teach that we live in a spiritual world. The power of God is above the power of evil. Evil always tries to place itself above the Most High's authority, even challenging God and accusing the brethren.

It is clear in the New Testament that people do fall away from the faith. They pay attention to deceitful spirits and believe doctrines of demons. Most in the Christian community think of those caught in witchcraft, sorcery, wizardry, magic, or astrology are *the* danger to the church. These are described as the works of the flesh and, for the most part, are not allowed to continue to prosper within a local congregation. In addition, they are usually associated with someone who does not have a relationship with Jesus Christ or someone who needs to be delivered from them. The biggest danger is when we find out that tares within the worldwide church often bring covert spiritual warfare that finally ends in persecution. In some mission enterprises, the name of God and even Christ are employed. Underneath the rhetoric and behind the scenes are demonic spirits in operation. That is why the apostle Paul mentions them in 1 Timothy 4:1: "But the Spirit explicitly says that in later times some will fall away from the faith, paying attention to *deceitful spirits* and *doctrines of demons*."

In his book *From Darkness to Light*, author Areon Potter describes this activity about deceitful spirits in his review of "How Satan and Demons Scheme Old Testament." He says,

> The thoughts they give a person are generally lies. Their purpose for lying is to cause the person to doubt God in some way. When we doubt God, we begin to trust in something else. At that time we become rebellious and disobedient to God (Job 4:17). Demons may impart some particular truth if it serves their purpose in adding weight to their deceptions.[19]

Deceitful spirits aid the false Christian mission by telling the leader or enterprise and those under their command to include God or Jesus in their doctrines or beliefs. The real result is that they do not trust God and use *sordid gain* for the acquisition of property or financial reward. Paul charges the church in 1 Timothy 6:17–18:

> Instruct those who are rich in this present world not to be conceited or to fix their hope on the uncertainty of riches, but on God, who richly supplies us with all things to enjoy. Instruct them to do good, to be rich in good works, to be generous and ready to share.

The use of money as Jesus and Paul describe it then is to channel money to operate the propagation of the gospel and not to reward oneself or a group of people with wealth. Those who seek money or fire people to gain others money are deceived. True believers need money to live. They should recognize that the first priority for which we use money is the accomplishment of sharing and communicating the gospel in the world. Under the disguise of Christian mission, the deceived and false gain personal wealth and prosperity. Wicked spirits are behind this, and you can be sure to find some fleshly sin from Galatians 5:19–21 working in the process as well.

There will always be those like Judas, Demas, the false disciples of John 6:66, and those often warned in Hebrews who abandon the faith.[20] There are those who make a deliberate departure from the true Christian belief, harming people intentionally, stealing money, and living the

"American dream" only to realize in the end that they are shipwrecked. The final position in eternity for apostates is "where the worm does not die and the fire is not quenched" (Mark 9:48).

Instead of cleansing and setting apart one's life as sacred (Jehovah-M'Kaddesh—a Hebrew name for God), deceitful *workers* who would claim they are Christian use money and prosperity to take advantage of true believers. Jesus told us, "You will know them by their fruits" (Matthew 7:16). In conclusion, we identify false workers by the following: "They do not love God, they do not have a pure heart, they have a warped conscious, and they have an insincere faith."[21]

Review: Deceitful Spirits and Doctrines of Demons

1. Lack of trust in God grants wicked spirits a legal right to oppose Christians (Romans 2:8).

2. Deceitful spirits may suggest and recommend that a religion following or including Jesus as God is the same as the relationship that His true followers believe. Demons simply imitate an intellectual agreement that Jesus and God are part of religion. They distort salvation by faith. Demons blind unbelievers to faith and trust in Jesus Christ alone for salvation (2 Timothy 3:5) and oppress Christians not to surrender all because of God's mercy to them (Romans 12:1).

3. Deceitful spirits control nonbelievers and some believers into keeping or obtaining money by robbing the true church (1 Timothy 6:9, Acts 5:1–11).

4. Deceitful spirits cause people who think they believe to fall away from the faith and ruin their lives. They counterfeit the work of God the Holy Spirit (Acts 5:3).

5. Doctrines of demons liberalize true salvation into merely head knowledge about the Christian faith. Doctrines of demons do not emphasize repentance and a changed life as true biblical Christianity. Doctrines of demons often bring recognition to someone other than Jesus Christ—for instance, Mother Mary or Muhammed or a famous world leader. God demands godly repentance, not sorrow from the world (2 Corinthians 7:10).

6. Principalities, powers, rulers, and wicked spirits' goal is to "steal, kill, and destroy" (John 10:10).

11

CHURCH DISCIPLINE AND THE PARACHURCH

WHAT IS CHURCH discipline? I have asked Christians what the process of church discipline is in the holy scriptures. To my disbelief, most do not know, and many find it to be a vague concept. It is a hard concept to apply because it is personal in nature. Jesus gave the process of reconciliation or church discipline in Matthew 18:15–17:

> If your brother sins, go and show him his fault in private; if he listens to you, you have won your brother. But if he does not listen to you, take one or two more with you, so that by the mouth of two or three witnesses every fact may be confirmed. If he refuses to listen to them, tell it to the church: and if he refuses to listen even to the church, let him be to you as a Gentile and a tax collector.

The only way these truths resolve any issues is for two people or two organizations to actually repent and forgive each other.

When people do not repent and forgive each other, evil-spirit beings get a legal right to oppose, deceive, oppress, and even control the organization or persons within that organization. We see how Judas had a form of godliness, but because he did not repent, he was deceived and used by Satan. He also trusted in money or *sordid* gain. "What are you willing to give me to betray him to you? And they weighed out thirty pieces of silver to him" (Matthew 26:15). Later on, Judas committed suicide, where he ended up in his own place. Suicide in Judas's case was the result of his neglect to rectify his life by godly repentance so he could have been reconciled to Christ and the ministry, as was Peter when he denied Christ.

The purpose of church discipline is restoration and edification. Church discipline is rarely practiced in local churches in the United States. It is even a rarer occurrence for local churches to confront their denomination or a parachurch ministry that has gone astray from solid biblical guidelines, especially concerning finances. This is not done because scandals may develop from a confrontation. They often produce large media coverage in the United States. The nonbelieving world exposes the lives of well-known actors but normally does not have an answer of how to restore such heroes to live a different life. The church generally faces either persecution or is laughed at when biblical restoration is attempted if it has gone public.

Christians already face persecution, harassment, being singled out or hounded when a pastor, a leader, or an organization fails. Since it is hard to convince the major portion of the world what repentance is—and we know that is the Holy Spirit's prerogative—it is unlikely that they would understand biblical restoration. Even Paul says it in Galatians 6:1, "Brethren, if anyone is caught in any trespass, you who are spiritual, restore such a one with a spirit of gentleness; each of you looking to yourself, so that you too will not be tempted."

The process of church discipline includes agreement of wrongdoing, repentance, growth, verification, and the restoration to the position one once held. Church discipline is to promote godly fear and purity in the church. In conclusion, the church has lost its power because of the following:

1. Many within the church are *tares*, just as Jesus told us in (Matthew 13:25).

2. Many Christians do not *self-evaluate* (2 Corinthians 13:5).

3. It is difficult to use church discipline on a group or on an individual outside a local congregation because it is easy to *distort* or *hide* the truth of the situation.

4. When church discipline has not been enforced, Satan and his forces have a *legal right* to continue to harass those involved in the situation (1 Corinthians 5:5, 1 Timothy 1:20).

5. Once a matter is determined to be resolved, or even if it is not resolved, *it should be left alone* by forgiveness. All those involved can move forward, and the Holy Spirit can bring conviction or consequences on the situation (Matthew 18:21–22).

Review: Church Discipline

1. Nonbelievers normally do not follow church discipline but often use its principles if it helps them gain something in worldly organizations (Matthew 18:23–35).

2. True believers must confess any known sin and attempt reconciliation to break deceiving spirits' legal right to oppress them. (1 John 1:9, Matthew 18).

3. God enforces His righteousness and holiness in the true church and expects it to move forward in power and love (Ephesians 4:30–32).

12

CHANGED LIVES
IN SCRIPTURE

As WE LOOK at the differences between a Christian and a nonbeliever, we see that several people in the New Testament were transformed by God the Holy Spirit as they believed in the Lord Jesus Christ. The important person of the Trinity involved in transforming these characters is God the Holy Spirit. They were willing to surrender all.

Apostle Paul

Paul was a member of the great Sanhedrin and was called Saul. He was an active leader in the persecution of early-century Christians. His goal was to eliminate Christianity. Paul reports to us that he was the chief of sinners after his conversion to Christ (1 Timothy 1:15).

His name was changed to Paul, his Roman name, and this was evidence of a change in his life. After his dynamic conversion, Paul shared the gospel around the known world. His purpose changed from eradicating Christians to preaching Christian salvation to the world. Paul did wrestle with the flesh as he wrote in Romans chapter 7, but he gave evidence that his life was changed.

Apostle Peter

Although a disciple of Jesus Christ, he offended Him in two ways. First, he tried to defend his Master by cutting off an ear of one of those trying to arrest Him named Malchus (Matthew 26:50–56). Secondly, he denied Christ after the arrest of Jesus took place (Luke 22:54–62).

After his conversion and transformation, Peter became a different man. He became known for his godly repentance and began preaching Christ crucified after the Holy Spirit was sent (Acts 2:38). He became a leader in the church and was eventually martyred for his faith in Jesus Christ.

Matthew

Matthew was a tax collector, his other name being Levi in scripture. Tax collectors in those days were thought to be rotten swindlers and sinners (Matthew 9:10). He was an apostle of Christ because he was a follower of Jesus, which meant he could not continue a habit of swindling people.

Zacchaeus

Zacchaeus was also a tax collector and a great sinner. He repented by saying that he would repay four times the amount if he had defrauded someone (Luke 19:1–19).

Review: Changed Lives

All four apostles had one theme in common: God changed their lives. It is obvious to us that when salvation is real in someone's life, they are changed. There is assurance of eternal life (1 John 5:10–13), and the changed life is evidence of the grace of God (Ephesians 2:8–9).

13

SUFFERING
IN THIS PRESENT AGE

WITHIN THE SOVEREIGNTY of God, suffering is part of God's program. Jesus the Christ became our example for suffering. "He was led as a sheep to the slaughter; And as a lamb before its shearer is silent, so he does not open his mouth" (Isaiah 53:7). As it was stated in an earlier chapter, suffering and death were the results of publicly testifying and confessing about the work and ministry of Jesus Christ. Early Christians suffered physical and emotional torture at the hands of evil and sinful leaders in Rome and in other places.

In the United States, we are often told that we as conservative Christians are not tolerant toward others. We are told we cannot read our Bible at work or pray at work, but most American Christians have not yet suffered torture or emotional pain like other countries. Our price for following God has not forced us into the challenges many Christians face in other parts of the world. Our faith has not truly been tested to such degree as of yet.

In the United States, we as Christians can affirm several obstacles to real revival. These all relate to the misunderstanding and purpose of suffering at the cross of Christ. Most godly men would agree that the following are substitutes for authentic revival: inertia of ease, the apathy of abundance, and the easy life as conformed to the world by many Americans. *Inertia* means "a resistance or declination to motion, action or change."[22]

Islam now is infiltrating our home country. It may seem small, but principalities and powers of darkness are often subtle in carrying out Satan's opportunity. Where we worked in Africa, there is a mosque on every corner just like there is a denominational church on every corner in the Southern United States. Perhaps soon, Islam will penetrate our society; and if God allows, it will take over our world to a degree. This could usher in the end-time. If we sleep and slumber—and even if we do not—it could be possible to see physical persecution here in the United States.

This persecution and suffering were not new to early Christians. *Foxe's Book of Martyrs* gives real-life accounts of how many evil men tried to eradicate the Christian faith. A group of Jews called in the apostles, and they flogged (skinned) the apostles and ordered them not to speak in the name of Jesus (Acts 5:34–41).

John Piper and Justin Taylor have written six key points that will help believers understand suffering in the context of persecution. These can be found in their book, *Suffering and the Sovereignty of God*: 1) Suffering deepens faith and holiness. 2) Suffering makes your cup increase. 3) Suffering is the price in making others bold. 4) Suffering fills up what is lacking in Christ's afflictions. 5) Suffering enforces the missionary command to go. 6) The supremacy of Christ is manifest in suffering.[23] *We* can make it more obvious by saying that many American Christians are lethargic, lazy, or idle. God uses suffering to get our attention.

Upon leaving Africa, my family and I felt emotionally rejected. However, we did not let the circumstances dictate how we were going to live for God. Following our assignment, God opened up a new ministry in another part of the world for us. "Nothing that comes to us from any source can injure us unless it causes us to have a wrong attitude."[24]

This was also true of Dietrich Bonhoeffer. Dietrich Bonhoeffer was resistant to the Nazi regime in World War II. He opposed Hitler's euthanasia program and genocidal persecution of the Jews. He was also arrested for planning to have Adolph Hitler assassinated. He preached throughout Germany. His sermons went all over Germany, and the Nazi knew that if they killed him, his shed blood would only confirm what he was preaching about the gospel during those hard times. He was eventually hanged after being in prison in a Nazi concentration camp only twenty-three days before the German surrender.[25]

> But even if you should suffer for the sake of righteousness, you are blessed. And do not fear their intimidation, and do not be troubled, but sanctify Christ as Lord in your hearts, always being ready to make a defense to everyone who asks you to give an account for the hope that is in you, yet with gentleness and reverence; and keep a good conscience so that in the thing in which you were slandered, those who revile your good behavior in Christ will be put to shame. For it is better if God should will it so, that you suffer for doing what is right rather than doing what is wrong. (1 Peter 3:14–17)
>
> Having been nine months in prison, Peter was brought from thence for execution, when after being severely scourged, he was crucified with his head downwards; which position, however, was at his own request. Previous to the death of St. Peter, his wife suffered martyrdom for the faith of Christ, when he exhorted her, as she was going to be put to death, to remember her Savior.[26]

Review: Suffering

1. Persecutions are part of following the teaching of the Bible from Apostle Paul and Peter (2 Timothy 3:10–11, 1 Peter 4:1– 2).

2. Early Christians thought it worthy to suffer for His name (Acts 5:41).

3. Persecution may bring about a kingdom movement (Matthew 5:1–16).

4. Christ's power is displayed in suffering against the conditions of human weakness, giving grace in place of escaping the circumstance (2 Corinthians 12:7–10).

5. God demands for Christians to do right in the midst of suffering (1 Peter 4:13–17).

14

THE CONGOS

As TIME WENT on, God called my family to Africa again. This time, it would be me, my son, and the president of the new mission going for a short term. We made plans to fly into the Republic of Congo, the Democratic Republic of the Congo and Chad. Both Congos are basically reached with established churches. Chad is in the 10/40 Window and has unreached people groups without an established church. The Dekakire, Baggara, and the Bagirmi Fulani are Islamic. Progress in reaching these groups is about 1.1 percent out of 100 percent as of 2013.

We landed in the Republic of Congo at Brazzaville after we left on Christmas Day. We began getting accustomed to the place. We stayed on the grounds of a hotel in tents. We pitched our tents on a cement slab, which was very uncomfortable, but the hotel manager did not charge us. He was remodeling areas of the hotel as it was closed down for Christmas holidays. Only at the end of our stay would we have one night in a real bed in the hotel.

I didn't know that I would be going to Congo where C. T. Studd and David Livingstone had been and first shared the gospel. It is amazing how God blessed me by allowing me to be in the area they preached. Remember, it was because of C. T. Studd's life and testimony that I became a missionary. C. T. Studd opened up the area called Pala Pala.

We needed to go across the Congo River into the Democratic Republic of Congo. The leaders of Sanda had originally offered us a property to develop our ministry work. So we would need to cross the river at Brazzaville over to Kinshasa and then take a six-hour drive to Sanda.

Before we did this, we went on tour to try to share *The Jesus Film* in French on the Congo Republic side. We rented a car for the time spent there. The owner of the rental car told us not to go to the Democratic Republic of Congo because they would kill us for money or for no reason at all. But that was why we went there—to get to Sanda in the Democratic Republic of Congo. I could tell demonic forces were already trying to produce fear of going there. We committed to prayer and went anyway. It's difficult to know that your friends, you, and your son could lose your life. But isn't that the call of the gospel? We may lose our lives physically, but Christians in the United States should already have discovered that "he who loses his life for my sake shall find it" (Luke 9:23–25).

Our first stop in the Congo Republic was a marketplace about twelve miles from where we were staying. It was called the Madibou Market. We attempted to share *The Jesus Film* on a white sheet as a screen with the new machine that operated on a simple chip. Due to sunlight, we couldn't show the film. The market was very busy, of about 7,500 people. This was my son's first observance of an African market. He had been a baby in our previous ministry years earlier in that other part of Africa. It was quite a shock to him with all the sour smells, the flies, and the overcrowding of people jammed into lean-to type of coverings. The smell of live fish mixed with improperly drained sewage and crowds of people made a lasting impression on him.

We shared the gospel with tracts, and I gave the gospel in French.

Through our stay, we were able to find a church at Lawool. We met with the pastor, Jean Paul, about sharing *The Jesus Film*. We made an appointment for a few days later. We were driving to the church, but we were very unfamiliar with the streets, which had no markings. We decided to stop at a gas station and ask directions. I asked a man on a motorcycle if he knew how to get to the church. He said yes. He said he would drive ahead of us until we knew more clearly where we had been earlier that week. But he just kept on driving his motorcycle until we pulled up at the church property. I got out of the vehicle and asked him if he was an angel. He said he didn't know. This was very unusual, but it was one of the miracles that God would perform for us on this trip.

We asked to meet with the pastor as we came into the church property. This was an evangelical church. The people were cordial and knew the powerful presence of the Holy Spirit. It took about fifteen minutes for the pastor to come out into the greeting room at his house. This was because he had malaria and was recovering from it. His children had been in the hospital as they had recovered from strong malaria.

We asked him if we could return and show *The Jesus Film*. We did that several days later. In front of the celebration building, the band was preparing for the next

Sunday service. There was electricity, so they were able to plug in the guitars. Along with the drums and the great singers, we heard "Praise be to God" in French. We set up *The Jesus Film*. Many stayed to the end, which was a great commitment. This was because it was dark at the end of the film, and they had to go home either on foot or get a ride of some sort in the dark.

The most powerful part of the event was when the women watching were wailing and crying as Jesus Christ was nailed to the cross. They had never seen the film before, and although already Christians, it made a profound effect on them, seeing the film. The Holy Spirit was very powerful there. The power of the Holy Spirit was unlike our weekly services in the States. He was overwhelmingly powerful. We even felt eyes watering as God confirmed the tremendous sacrifice of Christ crucified. I hadn't experienced such power since our previous missionary experience in West Africa.

We left after the film. We told the pastor we would be back to show the film if we had time. We never made it back there. We made plans to cross the great Congo River to go into the Democratic Republic of Congo.

It is very difficult for Christians in the United States to understand the difficulty of getting things done in Africa. Just to get tickets to cross the Congo River was a nightmare of a problem. First, the driver of the rental car, Gildas, had to find his friend, a point man, to get our stamps/visas to cross the river. Many point men harassed us to get the business.

You don't really know who to trust. He took our passports to the officials, got them approved, and returned them to us. You must understand that there is much bribery and underhanded application of money in Africa. Stealing by default is not uncommon. You must write down the price that you agree on, or they come back with other expenses and figures. That is why the cost to reach people in Africa is so high financially, and if you are not filled and controlled by the Holy Spirit, you would be most frustrated.

As we were in line to take the fifteen-foot motorboat across the Congo, a man came by and stole out of our president's handheld camera. We yelled out, and I yelled toward the ramp of the port that a robbery had taken place. "Voler, voler," I cried in French. The president rushed through the line on the ramp and got down to where the camera was in the hands of the man. He claimed to be a port official and that it was unlawful to take photos in this area. There were no signs or written evidence or oral evidence of this. The camera was finally returned after much talking with the "Duane's" officials.

As we were crossing the Congo River, a man sitting across from me became very worried. We had about twenty people in that small boat with all the luggage. The ride in the boat was very rough. We were overloaded. He kept saying, "We are overloaded," as if we were going to sink. It was not a luxurious ride. In fact, if you fell out, you would be swept away by the strong Congo current. I asked the man if he knew how to swim. He replied no. Then I asked him if he knew where he would spend eternity. He became even more nervous. Then I asked him if he believed there was a hell and where he would be going after physical death. He was so afraid that he couldn't answer those questions. This was just one of many times I shared the gospel.

The real nightmare was trying to get off the boat with our luggage. It was chaos in the tenth degree. All the people were pushing, shoving, and juggling with luggage for a position to move through customs. Pascal, an African friend of the president, was waiting to help us get through customs. Money was required, but there were not any set prices. So we spent another sixty dollars or so on customs. Pascal had an SUV waiting for us. They took us to the Meridian where we could discuss business costs about getting to the area we were to minister to about six hours away.

We made it to the property in Sanda in a two-wheel-drive vehicle, which later would be ruined. We pitched our tents and cleaned out one of the many old houses that the Belgians in the 1800s had built to live in. They exported bananas during that time and also exploited the people. As I was cleaning, spiders got into my tennis shoes. They bit seven big holes in my feet. In the United States, I would have to have them taken care of. Even the lab there didn't know exactly what caused the painful sores. They just put *arachnid* on the lab report. We had to filter water with a small hand pump. We ate hard-boiled eggs and camping backpack food. Mangos were available for free, but we paid for bananas. It was neither easy nor convenient to cook on coal. There was not any electricity or running water. The water was collected from the gutters of the roof and drained into a concrete holding tank. I spent hours pumping for six people to have filtered water.

We shared *The Jesus Film* several nights that we were there. Every morning, we called all the villagers to participate with us. We had the Bible on a recorder for them to listen to. We had service initially for the youth, but many came from all ages. We shared testimonies, sang gospel songs, and preached the message of salvation. This was done in French, Lingala, and Congolese. Many were curious. Two young men professed Christ, and one young man who was already a Christian participated with us more intensely.

The two young men who confessed Christ were drawn to salvation by my teenage son. Even though my son couldn't speak the language, the curiosity of the young people with him opened the way for us to share the gospel. I did so with them for about two hours. The next day, they confessed Christ. We tried to have a baptism, but the two-wheel-drive car had a hard time getting out of the four-wheel-drive property because it had rained. We were to meet them on the main road and have a baptismal service later. We were unable to meet with them. Yanik, Allen, and John were fruits of our labor.

The last day, we headed out to return to the capital city of Kinshasa, the Democratic Republic of Congo. The rain overnight made the jungle road very slick. We had to avoid areas of mud where holes filled with water blocked the road. We had the teens help push the car when it was stuck and unable to go up the rain-soaked hills. Yanik and Allen helped us push the car as needed the entire seven kilometers. They walked the whole way, often running to catch up until the car was stuck again. At the opening where the four-by-four roads ended and the pavement began, we stopped. Pascal gave them each the equivalent of two dollars for their hard work. We said our good-byes and hoped we would return to see them again someday.

We drove back to the capital city. Along the way, the car kept overheating. We stopped often to fill the radiator with water as it overheated. I believe the head gaskets were blown. And so it was finally we were stuck between Matadi and Kinshasa at 3:00 a.m., with a broken-down car. We waited until daylight to make attempts to make our return. Amazingly, a Christian man in a Gremlin offered to help pull the car up the long hill so that we might be able to drive on farther. The Africans cut out the seat belts out of our car to use as a towrope. Unfortunately, the Gremlin's clutch burned almost completely out. Finally we got a ride to the next town. We rented a vehicle to get back to the boat ramps—then across the Congo to fly to Chad from Brazzaville.

A goal had been accomplished. ICOR was now established in DRC through a national named Calvin. In summary, God the Holy Spirit had definitely moved. We saw people come to the broken-down school building to hear the gospel. God was real there in His strength and power because we saw how all ages of people were curious about what we were preaching—Jesus Christ and Him crucified (1 Corinthians 2:2).

Review: The Congos

1. The preaching of the gospel in all the world is done in obedience to our Lord Jesus's command (Matthew 28:18–20).

2. The power of the Holy Spirit was very present with us. The United States church has lost, for the most part, the emphasis, empowerment, and guidance of the Holy Spirit (John 16:7–14).

3. Remember, God loves all people.

4. C. T. Studd founded the Heart of Africa Mission, now known as WEC. He visited the Belgian Congo, now known as the Democratic Republic of Congo in1913, establishing eight mission stations. David Livingstone established the Livingstone Inland Mission from 1878 to 1884. These two made headway in the Congos in early missionary endeavors.

5. Bribery and theft are very common in Africa, which goes contrary to Holy Scriptures.

15

CHAD

From the Congos, we had to fly into the Cameroon airport to get a flight into Chad. We had no idea how, who, or what we would encounter there. Our baggage was lost in transit. We were planning on sleeping in tents, but all our gear was not with us. We had camping equipment, water filters, and other important information about our mission work. I had placed numerous tracts in French and Arabic in the suitcase to share, donated by a Christian discipleship organization. They were all lost. Upon arriving in Chad, we found the Hotel Le Central owned by Philippe Defranoux. We were able to purchase rooms and have a night of good sleep.

The next day, we began touring N'Djemena, the capital of Chad. We were leaning on God the Holy Spirit to guide us on what to do next because we knew no one personally in Chad. First we went to the American embassy to help us understand the basics of the country. Then we went to have our visa stamped to tour the countryside and to be able to take photos inland. We decide to go to CFAO Motors to try and rent a car for the stay. We determined the cost of obtaining a new four-wheel-drive Toyota loaded for future reference was about $80,000. There we met Maiimouna Moussa. He referred us to a relative of his, Ousman. Ousman became our chauffer for the rest of the trip, along with his uncle's, Badaoui Tidjani's, car. Badaoui Tidjani would take us to the nomads, the Baggara, and the camel herders.

Due to lack of finances raised in the United States, I slept in the rental car for three of the nights while in Chad. It was very uncomfortable for sleeping but safe and secure in the parking lot at Le Central. We finally found Team Mission. There we were able to rent rooms at a more reasonable price rather than spend money that we didn't have on hotel rooms. God the Holy Spirit had been speaking to me through the following scriptures:

> Vindicate me, O God, and plead my case against an ungodly nation; O deliver me from the deceitful and unjust man! (Psalm 43:1)

> You with your own hand drove out the nations; Then you planted them; You afflicted the peoples, Then you spread them abroad. (Psalm 44:2)

> But you have saved us from our adversaries and you have put to shame those who hate us. (Psalm 44:7, NASB)

Rise up, be our help, And redeem us for the sake of your loving-kindness. (Psalm 44:26)

God is our refuge and strength, A very present help in trouble. (Psalm 46:1)

The Lord of hosts is with us; the God of Jacob is our stronghold. (Psalm 46:7 and Psalm 46:11)

These scriptures read were essential to confirm that I was acting and working in God's will with confidence.

Through Ousman, we were able to meet his uncle Badaoui Tidjani. We mentioned the Baggara and the milk ministry to Ousman. He suggested contacting his uncle. He was a Muslim man, an engineer consultant. He also was raising cattle for milk. We went to his cattle farm to see the project he was working on. Before leaving the United States, we looked at the Baggara people on joshuaproject. net, hoping to make contact with them in Chad. They wander through Chad, being at different places during the seasons. They raise camels, use them to transport their living essentials, and sell their milk.

Badaoui was a Muslim person used by God to take us directly to the Baggara. This in itself is the divine intervention of God. Remember, we knew nobody personally in Chad. We took an hour drive to reach the area where he knew to find them. He spoke Chadian Arabic, as did the Baggara. So we made contact with them and took photos. Unfortunately, we could not share the gospel with them. Obviously, this was because Badaoui was Muslim and probably would not have translated God's message of salvation correctly. He was closed to the gospel. I had explained it to him over the days we were with him several times.

I met a Christian man named Nessie who was a waiter at Le Central. He was a channel that led us to the evangelistic church pastor in N'Djemena, the capital. We went to him to communicate our mission and calling to evangelism and orphans. There is an overwhelming number of orphans, street children, in Chad. He had one of his missionaries named Angel and a Christian driver take us to the town of Guelengdeng. The drive was one and one-half hours to get there. On passing through the dry area, I saw the Fulani people from the car window. We were told that elephants occasioned the area, but we didn't see any. Due to time restraints, we were not able to stop so that I could minister to the Fulani. What a blessing to recall memories of sharing the gospel with them in earlier missionary days. "And all the nations who are called by My Name, Declares the Lord who does this" (Amos 9:12).

Along the way, we stopped for lunch. Angel bought us sheep meat cooked right off the "grill." It was placed and rolled on rough brown paper used as a plate. It was nicely seasoned and warmly cooked. Along the route, he showed us where secular organizations had placed medical clinics, really small dispensaries, and some other work done.

Arriving in Guelengdeng, we were able to meet the leaders of the area. Several were pastors, and they had a small evangelistic work going on there. They said young Moslems played soccer with young Christians in the makeshift field, so at that point, there was not a lot of animosity between the two groups.

Seeking the Lord, we decided that there was an opportunity to pursue placing an orphanage there in Guelengdeng. The leaders were for us pursuing this project. They asked us back to the area as God leads. So now on our return to the United States, we would be pursuing the will of God for this challenging work.

Near the end of our stay, we went to the evangelistic church 14 of Chad. It was as if God was confirming our ministry. The pastor preached on Psalm 43. That is no coincidence but a supernatural work of the Holy Spirit in our lives. It is a wonder what God will do in the future.

Review: Chad

1. Biblical Christian faith missions believe that Jehovah-Jireh is able to intervene in circumstances, and all needs for the work will be provided as He sees the need. Jehovah-Jireh is He who sees the need and provides for it. God, Jehovah, will see to it (Gen. 22:14). Faith eliminates trust in self and creates absolute dependency on God the Holy Spirit to lead.

2. *Adonai* describes God as Lord and Master. All who come to know Christ as Master can enter into Christ's perfect rest and expect to receive from Him God's direction, supervision, and provision. Adonai is supreme authority (Malachi 3:1).

3. Jesus said in Mark 11:22, "Have faith in God." This references His supreme deity.

4. God will use ordinary Christians surrendered to El Shaddai to accomplish His work. Those Christians who are not totally surrendered are loved and accepted by God, they are used by God by His grace as instruments in righteousness (Revelation 4:8).

5. God, El Olam, is He who is the everlasting and has secrets to reveal to us. He has perpetual strength. This is why He guides in the Holy Scriptures and, in my case, in Chad (Psalm 41:13).

6. Jehovah-Shammah delights to be where his people are. Would God want to be where you are? Job commented, "Now I see thee" (Job 42:5).

7. It is the Lord who does all these things (Amos 9:11–12).

16

EVANGELISM: A HIGH WORK

GOD HAS SOVEREIGNLY chosen to provide North American Christians living in the United States with an abundance of Bible study tools. The United States is overflowing with Bibles, books, tracts, and Bible study materials. Jehovah-Jireh has provided for Christians all that is needed to prepare for the spiritual battle that exists in the world. Although much truth is available, at this writing, we have yet to see a Holy Spirit–empowered revival across our land since the 1980s. There may be pockets of transformed Christians, but generally, we see the world system taking over our blessed country. We will pray that our Christianity has not become a spectator sport. "There are not two Christs—an easy going one for easy going Christians and a suffering toiling, one for exceptional believers. There is only one Christ."[27]

Could it be, as it was for Israel, that "the glory of the Lord is departed" (1 Samuel 4:21, 22) from the church as a whole? *Ichabod* means there is "no glory or inglorious" (dishonorable).[28] What is needed is a return to trusting in the sufficiency of Almighty God. Trusting in self-sufficiency has created this lack of trust and power in the finished work of Jesus Christ on the cross and the Person and power of the Holy Spirit. One Hebrew name for God is Jehovah-Nissi.[29] The Hebrew word *nissi* comes from the Hebrew word *nac*, which means "to raise a banner a flag fluttering in the wind."[30]

> If we want to be victorious over the world, the flesh, and the devil, we must enter the battle under God's direction and banner. It is then we will experience supernatural power to accomplish His desires.[31]

We can see this in modern-day Christianity because it has left out the teaching of the cross, the burial, and the resurrection power of Christ Jesus our Lord.

Francis A. Schaeffer wrote tremendous truths in his *Complete Works* in two titles of his fivefold writings; *The Church at the End of the Twentieth Century* and *The Church Before the Watching World.* He gives an assessment of how the church might look in the days that we are now living in. In these works, he states how the church looks like the world.[32]

Not only is our country in need of revival but so is the world. Islam claims millions of followers in the 10/40 Window. The 10/40 Window is a rectangular area of North Africa, the Middle East, and Asia between ten degrees and forty degrees north latitude.

> This window includes historical and biblical significance, the least evangelized countries, the unreached peoples and cities, the dominances of three religious blocs, the preponderance of the poor, spiritual stronghold, and a renewed focus. (The Joshua Project)[33]

Few USA Christians are sacrificing their lives to go to these areas where trust in Almighty God is essential.

What can we do as Christians?

> We must recognize that Jesus is the King. The
> Holy Ghost is the governor. When you are saved,
> you receive the kingdom. You're grafted or adopted
> into the kingdom. The kingdom was manifest when
> Jesus was taken, stripped, crucified, died and rose
> again. The church (sons of God), the residents of
> the colony, was established on the day of Pentecost.[34]

Faith and presumption do not agree.

> In true faith, God is always the initiator, and man
> is always the responder. In presumption the order
> is reversed: Man assumes the role of initiator and
> tries to use 'faith' as a power to force God to be a
> responder![35]
>
> No Soldier in active service entangles himself in
> the affairs of everyday life, so that he may please the
> one who enlisted him as a soldier. (2 Timothy 2:4)

Religion deceives and withholds all those who would
give total allegiance to God Almighty into bondage. It is
a repulsive because it idolizes man instead of establishing
a personal relationship with God. The early church had a
dynamic relationship with the Triune God, and the world
during their lifetime did not have any doubts of it.

The primary purpose of the church is world evangelism.
This is not the only purpose, but many missiologists

and I believe it to be the primary purpose other than being conformed to the image of Christ. The process of understanding this may be as follows from, *The Ins and Outs of Rejection* by Dr. Charles Solomon.[36]

The Message of the Church   The Message of the Cross

The Message of the Church	The Message of the Cross
1. Conviction of sin (sinner)	1. Condition of self (flesh)
2. Saved from sin	2. Saved from self
3. Lordship within	3. Obedience to Christ—life
4. Assurance of salvation	4. Assurance of identification
5. Security (joy)	5. Security (victory)
6. Doubts (Satan)	6. Doubts (Satan)
7. Sins (1 John 1:9)	7. Self or flesh
8. Fellowship (church membership)	8. Fellowship with the Spirit's control
9. Service (leading souls to Christ)	9. Service (leading Christians to the cross)

Church As a Replacement for Christ

Instead of trying to get people to go to church, we should talk about Christ with those we meet in the world. The world in the United States knows about the church, and much of it is oftentimes negative. Many times, nonbelievers' excuse is that they do not want organized religion or hypocrisy. We should talk to people about the death, the crucifixion, the resurrection, and the ascension into glory of Jesus Christ. When someone gives us the opportunity to mention Christ, we should give our testimony. While working with Islam on frontline evangelism, we never talked about church. There were no churches yet, so that made it easier. We talked about the Old Testament saints like Abraham and Joseph. That process led to talking about a crucified, risen, and ascended Christ Jesus in the New Testament.

Fear: Apprehension and Terror

Improper fear in witnessing is the result of trusting in self-sufficiency. Fear grips many Christians because they may feel misunderstood and not accepted. They may also feel that their lives are not in order and fail to testify. This is another area of the flesh that needs to be taken under control by the Holy Spirit. The truth of the gospel does not rest on us. It rests in the work already accomplished by the Savior at his death, burial, resurrection, and ascension. *Jesus Christ stands for Himself.*

Improper fear in witnessing may lead to terror. *Terror* is "intense, overpowering fear."[37] Demonic forces take advantage of and oppress Christians in such a way that they feel afraid or fearful to share their faith when they know they can and have the power to do so. Romans 8:11 says,

"But if the Spirit of Him who raised Jesus from the dead dwells in you, He who raised Christ Jesus from the dead will also give life to your mortal bodies through His Spirit who dwells in you."

Thoroughly Established in the Faith: Redemption

Redeemed people must understand the price it cost our Savior Christ Jesus on Calvary's cruel cross.

> Blessed be the Lord God of Israel, For He has visited us and accomplished redemption for His people. (Luke 1:68)

> Christ redeemed us from the curse of the Law, having become a curse for us—for it is written, "CURSED IS EVERYONE WHO HANGS ON A TREE." (Galatians 3:13)

> So that He might redeem those who are under the Law, that we might receive the adoption as sons. (Galatians 4:5)

> Who gave Himself for us to redeem us from every lawless deed, and to purify for Himself a people for His own possession, zealous for good deeds. (Titus 2:14)

> And they sang a new song, saying, "Worthy are You to take the book and to break its seals; for You were slain, and purchased for God with your blood men from every tribe and tongue and people and nation." (Revelation 5:9)

> And they sang a new song before the throne and before the four living creatures and the elders; and no one could learn the song except the one hundred and forty-four thousand who had been purchased from the earth. (Revelation 14:3)

> These are the ones who have not been defiled with women, for they have kept themselves chaste. They are the ones who follow the Lamb wherever He goes. These have been purchased among men as first fruits to God and to the Lamb. (Revelation 14:4)

Discipleship is necessary if the church is going to be on the front lines of evangelism. This is why the church has teachers and growth studies. A panorama of the Bible; an understanding of salvation, sanctification, identification, the armor of God; and evangelism are important topics to master if the church is going to be evangelizing the world.

The Cross of Christ: The Appeal to Be Sold Out for Jesus Christ

1. The cross offers to set us free from the penalty of our sins.

    a. The cross covers my sins or washes them away

    b. The cross obtains pardon or forgiveness.

    c. The cross delivers me from the power of the enemy.

    d. Romans 3:23–24, 6:23; Romans 5:9–10; Ephesians 1:7; Hebrews 9:22; 1 Peter 1:19; 1 Corinthians 15:3–4

2. The cross sets us free from the power of sin.

    a. The cross crucifies my old nature.

    b. The cross obtains deliverance and victory.

    c. The cross is needed to crucify me, the sinner.

    d. The cross deals with sin, an unholy force or power that is in me but is not me.

    e. The cross is the instrument of death as a Christian understands discipleship.

    f. 1 Corinthians 1:30; Colossians 1:13; Galatians 2:20; Romans 6:3–23, 8:1–2; Ephesians 2:5–6; 4:22–24; Colossians 3:1–10, 3:12–17; Luke 9:23–26

The Holy Spirit: An Overlooked and Underestimated Person of the Trinity

The Holy Spirit is God, the person of the Trinity who guides us into all truth. It is the Holy Spirit that convicts the world of sin, righteousness, and judgment to come. It is the person of the Holy Spirit who gives power to the Christian to have victory over the flesh. It is the Holy Spirit who gives victory in the spiritual battle. It is the power of God by the Holy Spirit that brings revival and transformation to the church. You as a Christian are the carrying vehicle of the person of the Holy Spirit, and the power of God dwells in you. Every Christian must appropriate and use God's power for His purposes. It is Christ living in you by the power of the Holy Spirit that bears fruit to a lost and dying world. Through you, the gospel testimony is presented to all who do not believe.

> The final result of the call to war against the powers of Darkness is Revival! But the outcome of that revival, which will come as the result of the victory over Satan, is ascension triumph, the appearing of Christ, and the casting of Satan and his evil powers into the abyss.[38]

God's Program Will Not Be Thwarted

God's program has always been to share the gospel around the world. Divine power from God is always displayed against human wisdom as Christians understand it. Although the enemy, Satan, and fallen angels have been given temporary, limited power at the command of God, He has won the battle and is receiving glory from believers. We must praise God. The church must pray that revival will come and that He will add to the church day by day those who are being saved (Acts 2:47). Hallelujah! Hallelujah!

We must return to and understand biblical faith! Simply put, *faith* is—for all I trust him. Biblical faith is placed in an eternal person, God. We place our faith in the *true* and living God. We must have a pure zeal for the *glory of God*.

> For this reason it says, "Awake, sleeper, And arise from the dead, And Christ will shine on you." (Ephesians 5:14)

1. The *holy faith* was once for all handed down to the saints (Jude 3).

2. There is *power in the name of Jesus* that accomplishes faith to be a witness and walk in power (Acts 1:8, Matthew 28:18–20, Galatians 5:22–26).

3. *Unfruitful works of darkness* hinder faith (Ephesians 5:11).

4. *Faith* is the assurance of things hoped for, the conviction of things not seen (Hebrews 11:1).

5. *Faith is obedience*, and it is to be propagated to the nations (Romans 1:5).

6. *Faith* incorporates *sacrifice* (Mark 8:36–38).

7. *Faith* is *God's work* in us (Galatians 2:20).

8. *Boldness* is a result of being baptized and filled with the Holy Spirit (1 Corinthians 12:13, Acts 1:5, Ephesians 5:14–21).

The church is a winner when it appropriates faith. "The Lord says to my Lord: Sit at My right hand Until I make Your enemies a footstool for your feet." (Psalm 110:1).

How to Be Certain of Eternal Life

You must publicly and audibly confess Jesus as Savior and Lord.

> I tell you, but unless you repent, you will all likewise perish. (Luke 13:3)

> That if you confess with your mouth Jesus as Lord, and you believe in your heart that God raised Him from the dead, you will be saved; for with the heart a person believes resulting in righteousness, and with the mouth he confesses, resulting in salvation. For the Scripture says, *whoever believes in Hin will not be disappointed.* (Romans 10:9–11)

How to Surrender Your Life to God As a Christian

> Therefore I urge you, brethren, by the mercies of God, to present your bodies a living and holy sacrifice, acceptable to God which is your spiritual service of worship. (Romans 12:1)

Heavenly Father, I choose to totally commit my life to You. I choose to yield my will to You and to commit to Your will as You reveal it to me. I choose to yield all my rights to You. I choose to unconditionally surrender every part of my life, spirit, soul, and body to anything You choose to do with it. I recognize my total commitment cannot be taken back. Thank You for being committed to my commitment. All this I pray in the name, power, and authority of the Lord Jesus Christ. Amen.

Scripture Index

Ezekiel

11:19

13:6–9

Daniel

10:12–14

Malachi

3:1

Matthew

5:1–16

5:10

5:11

6.1–34

7:15`

7:16

9:10

10:26

10:28

10:34

18:23–35

10:35

12:28

13:25

18

18:15–17

18:21–30

18:2–22

26:15

26:54–62

26:50–56

28:15–20

28:18

28:19

28:20

Mark

5:1–20

8:36–38

9:48

11:22

11:25

Luke

1:68

9:23

9:23–25

9:23–26

9:25

9:26

11:20

13:3

19:1–19

22:54–62

John

3:3

6:7–14
6:63
6:66
10:3
10:10
14:6
16:7–14

Acts

1:5
1:8
2:38
2:47
5:1–11
5:3
5:34–41
5:41
9:15–16

Romans

1.5
2:8
3:23–24
5:9–10
5:17
6:3–23
6:6
6:1–23
6:22

6:23
8:1–2
8:11
8:14
8:16
10:9–11
12:1
12:2
12:1–2
14:12

1 Corinthians

1:18
1:30
2:2
5:5
6:9–11
7:10
12:10
12:13
15:3–4

2 Corinthians

5:17
7:10
7:7–10
10:3
10:4
10:5

SUBJECT INDEX

A

Adonai 9, 134
Alexander the Coppersmith
  88, 90, 91, 92
Allah 61, 78
Angel 120, 132
name for friend Gabriel 132
Angels 66, 132
Apostates 59, 100
Apostle 37
false 79
Apprehension 140
Assurance of Salvation 22

B

Baggara 117, 130
Bagirmi Fulani 130
Believer 106
Bible 18, 19, 61
Biblical 145

Big Valley 24
Bondage 21
Brokenness 29

C

Catholic 78
Catholicism 78
C.T, Studd 36, 127
Chad 129
changed life in 109
Christ, Jesus Christ 90
his Power 120
name above all names 71
the Christ 51, 62
the Messiah 62
our God 62
Church 101
local 101
para Church 101
purity in 101
Confession of Sin 146

BIBLIOGRAPHY

Ali, Abdullah Yusuf. *The Meaning of the Holy Quran.* Beltsville, MD: Amana Publication, 1997.

The American Heritage College Dictionary. 3rd ed. Boston: Houghton Mifflin Company, 2000.

Billheimer, Paul E. *Don't Waste Your Sorrows.* Minneapolis, MN: Bethany House, 2006.

Coleman, Robert. *The Master Plan of Evangelism.* Grand Rapids: Fleming H. Revell Company, 1972.

Foxe, John. *Foxe's Book of Martyrs.* Nashville, Tennessee: Thomas Nelson Inc., 2000.

Grubb, Norman. *C. T. Studd: Cricketer & Pioneer.* Fort Washington, PA: CLC Publications, 1982.

———. *Rees Howells: Intercessor.* Cambridge, UK: Lutterworth Press, 1952.

Holcombe, Steve. *Reformation and the End Time Anointing.* Canton, GA: Yawn's Publishing, 2010.

Joshua Project online at www.joshuaroject,net/10-40-window.php

MacArthur, John Jr. *First Timothy MacArthur New Testament Commentary.* Chicago, Illinois: The Moody Bible Institute of Chicago, 1995.

Maxwell, L. E. *Born Crucified.* Chicago, Illinois: Moody Press, 1945.

McDowell, Clyde. *How to Discover Your Spiritual Gifts.* Colorado Springs, US: Lay Action Ministry Program Inc., 1988.

Murray, Andrew. *The Prayer Life.* New Kensington, PA: Whitaker House, 1981.

Nee, Watchman. *Sit, Walk, Stand.* Mumbai, India: Gospel Literature Service, 1957.

Penn-Lewis, Jessie. *War on the Saints.* New Kensington, PA: Whitaker House, 1996.

Piper, John and Justin Taylor. *Suffering and the Sovereignty of God.* Wheaton, Illinois: Crossway Books, 2006.

Schaeffer, Francis. *The Complete Works of Francis Schaeffer. A Christian World View, 5 Volumes.* Wheaton Illinois: Crossway Books and Bibles, 1988.

Solomon, Charles R. *The Ins and Outs of Rejection.* Lancaster, UK: Solomon Publications, 1991.

Strong, James. *Strong's Exhaustive Concordance of the Bible.* Peabody, Massachusetts: Hendrickson Press, 2009.

NOTES

1. *The American Heritage College Dictionary*, 3rd ed. (Boston, Massachusetts: Houghton Mifflin, 1993), 1386.

2. Charles Solomon, *The Ins and Outs of Rejection* (Lancaster, UK: Solomon Publications, 1991), 163.

3. Elisabeth Elliot, preface to *Under the Shadow of the Almighty* (London: Hodder & Stoughton, 1958), 6.

4. Jack R. Taylor, *Prayer: Life's Limitless Reach* (US: Burkhart Books, 2004), 158.

5. Watchman Nee, *Sit, Walk, Stand* (Mumbai, India: Gospel Literature Service, 1957), 78.

6. Andrew Murray, *The Prayer Life* (New Kensington, PA: Whitaker House, 1981), 2.

7. Ibid., 13–17.

8. Taylor, *Life's Limitless Reach*, 11.

9. Unless otherwise noted, definitions used in this book are found in *The American Heritage College*

Dictionary, 3rd ed. (Boston, New York: Houghton Mufflin Company, 2000), 20.

10. Abdullah Yusuf Ali, *The Meaning of the Holy Qur'an* (Beltsville, MD: Amana Publication, 1997), 251.

11. Ibid., 9.

12. Ibid., 239.

13. Ibid., 1181.

14. Ibid., 126.

15. James Strong, "Greek Dictionary of the New Testament," in *Strong's Exhaustive Concordance of the Bible* (Peabody, Massachusetts: Hendrickson Publishers Inc., 2009).

16. Clyde McDowell, *How to Discover Your Spiritual Gifts* (Colorado Springs, US: Cook Communication Ministries International, 1988), 20–24.

17. Steve Holcombe, *Reformation and the End Time Anointing* (Canton, GA: Yawn's Books & More Inc., 2010), 280.

18. *The American Heritage College Dictionary*, 1387.

19. Areon Potter, *From Darkness to Light: Demonic Oppression and the Christian* (Mustang, OK: Tate Publishing Inc., 2006), 48.

20. John MacArthur Jr., *First Timothy MacArthur New Testament Commentary* (Chicago, Illinois: Moody Publishers, 1995), 147.

21. Ibid., 148.

22. *The American Heritage Collegiate Dictionary Third Edition*, (page 695).

23. John Piper and Justin Taylor, *Suffering and the Sovereignty of God* (Pages 91-109).

24. Paul E. Billheimer, *Don't Waste Your Sorrows*, (page 92).

25. Wikipedia, Summary of the article on Dietrich Bonhoeffer.

26. John Foxe, *Foxe's Book of Martyrs* (page 9).

27. Hudson Taylor, *Hudson Taylor's Spiritual Secret*, (Page 237).

28. James Strong, Strong's Exhaustive Concordance of the Bible, Hebrew, and Chaldeen Dictionary, (page 11, #350).

29. James Strong, *Strong's Exhaustive Concordance of the Bible*, (page 47, #3071).

30. James Strong, Strong's Exhaustive Concordance of the Bible (page 79, # 5251).

31. Areon Potter, *from Darkness to Light*, (page 207).

32. Francis A. Schaeffer, *The Complete Works of Francis Schaeffer, 5 Volumes*.

33. *Joshua Project* on line at www.joshuaproject,net/10-40-window.php.

34. Dr. Steve Holcombe, Reformation and The End Time Anointing, (pages 43, 44).

35. Areon Potter, *from Darkness and Light*, (page 235).

36. Dr. Charles Solomon, *The Ins and Outs of Rejection*, (pages 73, 76).

37. The American Collegiate Dictionary Third Edition, (page 1401).

38. Jessie Penn-Lewis, *War on the Saints*, (page 324).

P113
P114

CPSIA information can be obtained
at www.ICGtesting.com
Printed in the USA
LVOW04s0751200916
505311LV00001B/2/P